M. K GANDHI AND THE SOUTH AFRICA

M. K GANDHI AND THE SOUTH AFRICA

INDIAN PROBLEM

P. J. METHA

Published by

FacsiMile Publisher
12 Pragati Market
Ashok Vihar, Ph-2
Delhi - 110052, India
Phone: 011-47034999
Email: www.facsimilepublishers.com
info@facsimilepublishers.com

Distribution Network
gyanbooks.com
India, USA, Canada, UK, Australia

ISBN: 978-93-7106-689-1 (PB)

First Published, 1910

2nd Impression 2025

Printed at: Gyan Press, Delhi.

M. K GANDHI AND THE SOUTH AFRICA
Arthur P. J. METHA

M. K. GANDHI

AND

THE SOUTH AFRICAN INDIAN PROBLEM.

——:o:——

INTRODUCTORY.

THIS is a dissertation mentioning a few of the incidents in Mr. Gandhi's life. It is not a biography in any sense of the term. It does not aspire to supersede that most fascinating life of Mr. Gandhi, which Rev. J. G. Doke placed before the public in 1909, or the one that was published last year by the enterprising firm of Messrs. G. A. Natesan & Co. It makes hardly any mention of the incidents in Mr. Gandhi's life that have been so well described in the above-mentioned books. It gives no dates of even the principal events of his life-time, not even the dates of his birth or marriage, his first landing in London or Durban. For a connected account of his life, the reader is requested to refer to the said books. This brochure is written particularly with a view to popularise those books, and might in some respects serve as a supplement to them. Having had a very long acquaintance with Mr. Gandhi, I am in a position to give an account of some of his characteristics, with which I am personally acquainted. In this, the reader will find an account of the further stages of progress of the struggle that has gone on in the Transvaal subsequent to the publication of those books. I wish in this brochure to show my appreciation of the noble stand that our Indian brethren in the Transvaal have made against tremendous odds in such a distant and unsympathetic land for over four years without intermission. I also wish to show my appreciation of the man who has led the campaign so successfully during the whole of that time. He has made the Transvaal Indian cause his own, and has sacrificed at its altar,—all that one prizes most in this mortal life. It is his brain that has conceived it possible for the Transvaal Indians to carry on a bloodless struggle to a successful and glorious end, and it is his personal example that has kept up the spirits of the fighters throughout that long period. He is so much identified with the struggle, that to mention one without mentioning the other is an impossibility. The story of the South African Indian Problem is almost the story of Mr. Gandhi's life.

In reviewing the life of Mr. Gandhi written by Mr. Doke, the *Transvaal Leader*, one of the leading newspapers in the Transvaal, in its issue of the 10th January, 1910, said :—

Any South African, if asked to name the public man of highest personal character in South Africa, would say that there was at any rate none known to him more favourably in that respect than Mr. Gandhi, the leader of the Asiatic passive resisters. It is about this individual whose personality has become widely heard of in the United Kingdom and India, as well as in this country, that Mr. Doke has produced the well-written book now before us. Apart from their relation to a political question, its pages are well worth a perusal for their human interest.

Every thoughtful Indian will be proud to read the appreciative remarks in the above extract coming from such an unexpected quarter, and to learn on how high a pedestal his countryman—the very same person who is known over there as the prime breaker of the Asiatic Registration and Immigration Restriction laws of the Transvaal, thereby placing the Government thereof in an awkward position—stands in the estimation of some of the Europeans in that Colony. In placing the short but masterly written life of our distinguished countryman before the public, Mr. Doke has earned the best thanks of the people of this country.

It is generally believed in this country that the white population in the Transvaal is very bitter against the Indians residing in that Colony. No doubt, there is a large number of politicians and others who are, in and out of season, trying to foster racial prejudices and jealousies and depicting the Indians in the blackest of colours. But at the same time it must not be forgotten that there are individuals there who are in full sympathy with the Indians and some of whom are devoting their time, energy and even money in their interests. Mr. Doke belongs to the latter category. He is one of the best friends of the Indians in the Transvaal. From the very commencement of the passive resistance struggle in the Transvaal in 1907, when he first came in touch with Mr. Gandhi, down to this day, he has stuck to them at great personal sacrifice, and rendered very valuable services to the cause.

There is a goodly number of the Transvaal whites who are ashamed of the various acts of injustice done to the Indians in South Africa. Mr. Doke is not only ashamed of the ill-treatment meted out to them, but he has all along consistently borne more than his share of the struggle quite nobly. In July of 1909 when Mr. Gandhi was deputed by the Transvaal Indian community to go to England to rouse the conscience of the British public, and Mr. H. S. L. Polak, the Editor of the *Indian Opinion* and one of the most feeling young Englishmen, was sent to India, to wake up the lethargic Indians to perform their duty towards their suffering brethren in the Transvaal, Mr. Doke cheerfully undertook to fill in the gap as Editor; and so ably did he guide the struggle and conduct the paper, that the absence of the principal workers from the field of operation was not much felt.

In writing the life of Mr. Gandhi, Mr. Doke's main object is to place before the world a graphic account of the disabilities the Indians are suffering from in the Transvaal and other British Colonies, to bring about a better understanding between the Colonists and Indians, and to have the status which the latter are to enjoy in the British Colonies and possessions determined once and for ever. To put it in his own words, at page 9 of the book, addressing Mr. Gandhi he says as follows :—

> Listen. It appears to me that what we are doing now is merely tinkering at the Asiatic settlement—our fight with this Government is only part of a much greater fight, to be fought out on a larger battle-field. The question of the status of British Indians throughout the whole empire will have to be solved, and in the settlement of this vast problem, you should have much to say. The question is how can we best prepare for that future.

To any one who has closely followed the struggle carried on in the Transvaal during the last four years, it is evident that its real object is, what is so tersely put by Mr. Doke in the above extract. Although it does not seem as if the struggle is going to come to an end soon, there are good grounds to believe that it has not been quite fruitless. Before the struggle the white colonists in South Africa used to look upon the Indians as so many coolies. An Indian Barrister used to be styled a coolie Barrister, a Doctor a coolie Doctor, a trader a coolie trader, and so on. But since the struggle, a vast change has taken place in their behaviour towards them, and the Indian settlers are now spoken of as British Indians. It would be to the interests of the country if the racial prejudices, so detrimental to both, were to dwindle down, and the two races were to live side by side as fellow subjects of the same empire.

POSITION OF INDIANS IN THE TRANSVAAL.

Mr. Doke has written Mr. Gandhi's life expressly for English readers. For the benefit of the Indian readers of this masterly production, it would not be out of place if I were to give a short summary of the main question, and the nature of the passive resistance movement as it had been carried on there for the last four years. Having been in that country in the year 1898, I have had an opportunity of studying the Indian problem as it then was; and since then I have been trying to keep myself informed of what is going on there.

In most of the British Colonies various laws have been passed with a view to prevent the immigration of Asiatics there. Australia, Canada and South Africa have taken the lead in the matter and have vied with one another in making each successive law as stringent as circumstances permitted them. These Colonies, in the course of the last twenty-five years, have created an amount of bitterness against the brown, the yellow and the black races in consequence of which the races of the West and the East are being driven almost into hostile camps. The main object of the various Immigration Restriction Acts of these Colonies is to hermetically seal their doors against any future ingress of the civilized peoples of India, China and Japan. Those, who are already settled down there, are denied all rights of citizenship. They are debarred from voting at Parliamentary and Municipal elections. Their merchants are put to innumerable hardships in the conduct of their business, and they find it very hard, year by year, to get their licenses renewed. In the Transvaal, there are additional hardships. They cannot acquire land to build their houses upon, they are not allowed to walk on the foot-paths, they are not allowed to travel in tram-cars, and they find it very hard to obtain tickets to travel on their Railways in the upper classes and in the Mail trains. The rulers of the Transvaal desire to place even the cultured Indians on the same footing as the ignorant Kaffirs on account of the colour of the skin. It cannot be denied that the colour prejudice has been carried too far in the Transvaal.

Lord Lansdowne, the late Viceroy of India, and the present leader of the Unionist Party in the House of Lords, in a speech delivered by him at Sheffield in 1899, just on the eve of the Great War in South Africa, expressed his great indignation at the treatment meted out to the Indians in the Transvaal. He said :—

> Among the many misdeeds of the South African Republic, I do not know that any fills me with more indignation than its treatment of the Indians. And the harm is not confined to sufferers on the spot; for what do you imagine would be the effect produced in India when these poor people return to their country to repeat to their friends that the Government of the Empress, so mighty and irresistible in India, with its population of 300,000,000, is powerless to secure redress at the hands of a small South African State.

Lord Lansdowne was not alone in feeling so strongly on the position of the Indians in the Transvaal. Most of those, who studied the grievances of the Indians in those days, were in full sympathy with them. The harsh treatment, to which the Indians were subjected during the Boer regime, was made one of the grounds for the declaration of war with the late Republic.

The British Resident at Pretoria was their best friend and did all that he could to ameliorate their condition. While at Cape Town, I paid a visit to the Private Secretary to Lord Milner, the then Governor of Cape Colony, and requested him to give me a letter of introduction to the Resident at Pretoria, with a view to obtain the necessary help from him if I should be put to any trouble while travelling in the Transvaal. He gladly furnished me with the necessary papers, and desired that in the event of any trouble being caused during my sojourn, I should report it to him directly. I am glad to say that my journey was unattended by any such mishap as I had feared. But now that the British flag is flying in that country, it would be quite different, if I wanted to make another trip to that country. In the first place, before crossing the Transvaal border, I shall be asked, and for the matter of that even the best of Indians would be asked, to produce a registration certificate according to Law 36 of 1908. This requisition must be complied with by every Asiatic whether he wishes to settle down in the country, or whether he is a temporary sojourner. Of course, in the latter case, the difficulties would not be quite so great as in the former. It is now a matter of notoriety that the Indians in the Transvaal had far fewer troubles in the days of the South African Republic than they have had during the regime established after the great Boer War.

The root of all the hardships and troubles from which the Indian population in the

Transvaal is suffering, is the Law No. 3 of 1885 passed by the late Republic. Among other things it enacted that :

They (the so-called coolies, Arabs, Malays, and Mahomedan subjects of the Turkish Dominion) shall not be capable of obtaining burgher (political or municipal) rights of the South African Republic and that they may not be owners of fixed property in the Republic except in such streets, wards, and locations as the Government shall appoint for sanitary purposes as their residence.

It also enacted that those who settled in the Republic for the purpose of carrying on trade, should register their names, and pay £ 25 once and for ever. Two years after, it was reduced to £3. The object of the law was not to prohibit Asiatic immigration, but to reduce trade competition. Before the War, the total Indian population in the Colony was 15,000 and the Chinese population 3,000. But immediately on the termination of the War, various regulations were issued from time to time to restrict their entrance into the Colony, and on the top of them all, was introduced that ill-fated law—the Registration Law of 1907—which further reduced the Asiatic population. At the present day there are not more than 5,000 Indians and 1,000 Chinese in the whole of the Transvaal.

On the success of the British arms and the re-establishment of a settled government after the demise of the late Republic, the old Law above mentioned, which was almost a dead letter during the Kruger regime, was, as it were, unearthed, and began to be enforced with the usual British precision and strictness. The result of it was that the few Asiatics who still resided in the Colony were harassed in a number of ways and most of them completely ruined. Referring to their present condition, Mr. Polak in his book on "The Indians of South Africa" gives a very graphic picture of the straits to which they are reduced. He says:—

> It is a record of shame and cruelty that has no counterpart within the confines of the British Empire. These things may be expected in Russia or in some other despotically ruled country, but not under the British flag, where, nevertheless, they occur. The lesson is one of faith, betrayed and broken pledges, bitter humiliation, cruel slander, strong hatred, vindictive revenge, sudden ruin, sometimes even of dispersed families, abandoned children, dishonoured women, emasculated men. The iron has eaten deep into the souls of the South African Indians. After years of unparalleled thrift, arduous toil, intense self-sacrifice, they have seen their-all snatched from them in the twinkling of an eye—as though an earthquake had suddenly come upon them, the earth had yawned, and had swallowed up the results of their labours. Brought up in awe and reverence of the power of the British Raj to protect the helpless and succour the weak, they see it powerless to secure the very relief from its own subjects that it sought for them at the cannon's mouth ten years ago from a small semi-independent State governed by an oligarchy of farmers ridden with an ignorant provincialism.

If the Law No. 3 of 1885, which was since its enactment strenuously resisted by the Imperial authorities from being put into actual operation, had been repealed on the establishment of British power in the country, as was hoped for by every friend of India and the Empire, the whole of the trouble that subsequently ensued would have been avoided. But no such thing was done or even attempted. During the late President Kruger's regime, the Indians used to get every kind of help and sympathy from the British Resident at Pretoria, but, there being none now to take his place, they are cruelly reminded of the comparatively happy days of the old regime.

On the termination of the War, Lord Roberts had a list of the old Indian settlers made out, and in due course permitted them to return to the Colony. He promised them that, on the pacification of the country, their grievances would be inquired into and redressed. But no sooner was this said than some of the white colonists, who feared Indian trade competition, began to agitate against their return to the country, and their agitation is still going on. In consequence of this, their former grievances remain unredressed up to the present day, and over and above that, they have lost the few rights and privileges they enjoyed during the pre-War days. The present policy of those in power is to prohibit altogether any further Asiatic immigration into the Colony and to drive out the old residents. When Superintendent Vernon, while giving evidence before a Magistrate, declared that "*I think it is a white man's duty to hunt these people out of the country*," he was probably voicing the intention of General Smuts and his colleagues. The Magistrate objected to his statement and his attitude. But the man is still holding the office that he occupied when he made that statement.

Referring to the Asiatic question in its usual strain *Volkstem*, the Transvaal Government organ, not long ago wrote as follows :—

> It must not be so easy to be delivered from the Asiatics. What exertion did it not cost us to be delivered from the Chinese (labourers)? And did that exertion not make our people stronger? The same will have to be the case in connection with the Asiatics. That South Africa will free itself from this exotic element, there can be no doubt. But it will cost many a drop of perspiration. When at last the Asiatic has been driven out, South Africa shall be all the better and more robust for it.

The Law 2 of 1907 and 36 of 1908 were enacted with the above objects in view. By virtue of these laws those Asiatics who have obtained the right of residence in that country, are obliged to get their names registered before the Registrar of Asiatics, to give their thumb and finger impressions, and to obtain a certificate from him. Any Police officer can ask any Asiatic to produce the certificate at any time, and those who cannot or will not produce it can be immediately hauled up before a Magistrate, and after a trial, sentenced to three months' hard labour or a fine of £100. Those who enter the country before providing themselves with the certificate as mentioned above, can be deported, in the first instance, by the order of the Executive Government, and those who re-enter after the said deportation ceremony is gone through, can be hauled up before a Magistrate and sentenced to six months' hard labour, or a fine of £100. Since the above laws were passed, no fewer than 3,500

Indians have suffered imprisonment, invariably with hard labour in the Transvaal prisons. Over and above this a large number of men have been illegally deported to India through the Portuguese territory. These men were entitled to stay in the country, and subsequently proved their right of domicile in it. Some of those valiant men were deported with no more than the articles of daily requirement they had with them, when they were arrested, and thus they suffered innumerable privations and sufferings while they were shifted from place to place. Some of them have had to leave their families behind, unprotected and uncared for. Fortunately, the little band of passive resisters under the leadership of Mr. Gandhi did what it could for them.

Before the King's sanction was given to the law of 1907, the Provisional Government of the Transvaal had passed the very same law. On the 11th of September 1906, a mass meeting of the Indians was called in Johannesburg to consider what steps they were to take on the law being allowed by the Imperial Government. It was attended by about 3,000 persons. The principal resolution passed at the meeting was that if the Indians were called upon to give marks of identification once more they would refuse to do so, and would instead submit to the penalties imposed by that law. The struggle has been going on ever since. During the four years of its continuance, various tragic scenes have taken place, and most of the leaders of the various Indian communities such as

Messrs. Gandhi, Dawood Mahomed, Rustamji Jivanji, Imam Abdul Kadar, Ahmed Mahomed Cachalia, Ibrahim Aswat, Thambi Naidoo and others, all highly respected in that country, have had to go to jail because they refused to give their thumb and finger impressions before the Police as required by the Asiatic Laws. Several Indians who took a prominent part in the struggle have been incarcerated in prison more than half a dozen times till now.

The Asiatic passive resisters in the Transvaal have no personal objects to serve in carrying on the struggle. They are simply fighting for the good name of India. These men think that if they quietly submitted to the Law, and neglected to perform their duty to their country on this occasion, they would be looked upon as a disgrace to the country that gave them birth. Instead of being carried away by wild notions of violence, which a small number of them would have liked to resort to, they made up their mind to suffer in their persons the penalties imposed by Law, and thus helped their country to maintain its sacred traditions and realise its glorious past. The *Rangoon Gazette* of the 9th December 1909 commended the struggle and the strugglers in the following terms :—

For the present, no right-thinking man will deny the fairness of the Indian claims. The force of the movement lies in its legitimate and constitutional character, and it is impossible to withhold approbation from men such as many of the Transvaal Indians have proved themselves to be. Their pertinacity, their moral fibre, and their self-sacrifice make up the chapter of history of which Indians will be proud. The Transvaal

Indians deserve every help from the various communities in India, that can reasonably be given.

THE PASSIVE RESISTANCE STRUGGLE.

In this place, I propose to give a short summary of that memorable struggle, in favour of which, men of almost all parties and views have unhesitatingly expressed so strongly. But before doing so, it would be better to give the genesis of it in the words of Mr. Gandhi. He has put it very neatly in an address that he delivered before an audience of Europeans at the Germiston (Transvaal) Literary and Debating Society in 1909. He said :—

Passive resistance was a misnomer. But the expression had been accepted as it was popular, and had been for a long time used by those who carried out in practice the idea denoted by the term. The idea was more completely and better expressed by the term "soul force." As such it was as old as the human race. Active resistance was better expressed by the term "body force." Jesus Christ, Daniel and Socrates represented the purest form of passive resistance or soul force. All these teachers counted their bodies as nothing in comparison to their soul. Tolstoy was the best and brightest (modern) exponent of the doctrine. He not only expounded it, but lived according to it. In India, the doctrine was understood and commonly practised, long before it came into vogue in Europe. It was easy to see that soul force was infinitely superior to body force. If people in order to secure redress of wrongs, resorted to soul force, much of the present suffering would be avoided. In any case, the wielding of this force never caused suffering to others. So that, whenever it was misused, it only injured the users, and not those against whom it was used. Like virtue, it was its own reward. There was no such thing as failure in the use of this kind of force. "Resist not evil" meant that evil was not to be repelled by evil, but by good ; in other words, physical force was to be opposed not by its like but by soul force. The same idea was expressed in Indian philosophy by the expression " freedom from injury to every living thing." The exercise of this doctrine involved physical suffering on the part of those who practised it. But it was a known fact that the sum of such suffering was greater rather than less in the world. That being so, all that was necessary, for those who recognised the immeasurable power of soul force, was consciously and deliberately to accept physical suffering as their lot, and, when this was done, the very suffering became a source of joy to the sufferer. It was quite plain that passive resistance, thus understood, was infinitely superior to physical force, and that it required greater courage than the latter. No transition was, therefore, possible from passive resistance to active or physical resistance. . . . The only condition of a successful use of this force was a recognition of the existence of the soul as apart from the body, and its permanent and superior nature. And this recognition must amount to a living faith, and not a mere intellectual grasp.

The passive resistance struggle as it has been carried on in the Transvaal, and the noble stand that the Indians have been able to make so far, by using it as their weapon to fight for their rights, has served to show to the world that after all physical force, however great, is not always capable of offering permanent resistance to the soul force of even a few individuals, if the object of the fight is altruistic. The States in which unjust and oppressive laws could with impunity be passed and administered high-handedly, regardless of the interests of even the meanest of their subjects, white, brown or black, cannot for long maintain their hegemony amongst nations. Speaking to a large and influential gathering at Johannesburg in 1906, on the differential treatment meted out to any one class of its subj-cts in any State, Lord Selbourne, the late High Commissioner of South Africa, made some very trenchant remarks. He said :—

> Injustice and oppression, as with a hot iron, sear the character of the people who oppress, and of the people who are oppressed. In the case of the oppressor, the effect is always and altogether evil. The oppressor passes from brutality to brutality, loses more and more the consciousness of his responsibility to God and sympathy for his fellow man. Men reap what they sow,
>
> " The mills of God grind slowly,
> But they grind exceedingly small."
>
> and right retribution one day meets the nation, the nation of the oppressor. Nor does the oppressed go unscathed. In his weakness, he takes refuge in falsehood, treasuring revenge. But also noble characteristics are drawn out and stamped on him. He becomes united under the political and social pressure with which he meets. He becomes pertinacious to a degree which elevates pertinacity to a public virtue, and he becomes capable of infinite self-sacrifice for his people, and his own kith and kin.

According to the saying that it is the last straw that breaks the camel's back, the Transvaal Indians went on for a great many years bearing the load of a number of disabilities they were subjected to in that country, and, perhaps, would have gone on like that indefinitely with mere grumblings coming out of their mouths. But as soon as the iniquitous Registration Law (here the saying does not quite apply, because the latter alone is a greater load than all the disabilities combined) was proposed to be added to it, they at once felt that they would have to succumb under its weight, if it was allowed to be added to the burden they were already carrying. Thus came about that memorable passive resistance campaign in that country. The Indians at once saw the folly of taking everything lying down; they therefore worked themselves up to the height of their manhood, in order to meet the new conditions. If they had quietly submitted to this Law, the Cape Colony, Natal and other Colonies under the British flag would have followed in its wake with similar laws, with the result that the Indians would have found the doors of the greater part of this earth closed against them before long. They have, in fact, saved the situation. There is still a large number of Indians, in this country as well as outside, who have failed to grasp the real meaning of the Transvaal Indian struggle. These would do well to go through Mr. Doke's book. It would show them that in carrying it on, they have taken the only manly course it was open for them to adopt, under the peculiar circumstances in which they were placed, and in so doing, they rendered inestimable services to India. The Transvaal Indians declare, and rightly too, that passive resistance is an infallible weapon against the unjust and oppressive laws of the States in which they live, and that there is no peaceful weapon so potent against the wrongful acts of States towards their subjects, as that of passive resistance. They have kept it on for four years, and are determined to carry it on until the Government accedes to their demands. The name of Mr. Gandhi will remain permanently associated with passive resistance, whenever and wherever it may be carried on hereafter.

Mr. Doke has written an excellent book in a small compass. His style is terse and forceful. He has managed to give in a short space of about 100 pages, a very vivid account of the self-sacrifice, self-control and self-renunciation of Mr. Gandhi in carrying on the above struggle as well as during the various phases of life through which he has passed. Mr. Gandhi's views on religion and ethics as narrated by Mr. Doke are also bound to commend themselves to a large number of its readers of all classes. Indians, however, will see in him a hero to their liking, and are bound to love him and admire the pure and gentle life that he has been living, the like of which they find depicted only in their ancient sacred literature. Worthy to be reckoned as one of the great men India has produced, this young Indian has, during the last seventeen years in a far-off land, cheerfully borne on his shoulders a load under which most leaders would have been overpowered. The pertinacity with which he has maintained his fights throughout has astonished the on-lookers and softened even the hardest of hearts. The troubles and hardships which the Transvaal Indians have suffered and are suffering, are now known all over the world, and the South African Indian question has long ago passed from the stage of parochial politics to one of high Imperial concerns. The little band of passive resisters, in fighting out its bloodless battle, has earned a reputation, similar to that a band of heroes enjoy after triumphs in bloody battles. The reputation for bravery which the Boers have acquired as fighters will, certainly, be tarnished, if they fail to recognize in this band, a similar virtue though in a far different spirit. Signs are not wanting to show that such appreciation will not be long in coming. The seeds of self-sacrifice planted by Mr. Gandhi in 1893, are beginning to bear fruit after 17 years.

During the continuance of the struggle in the Transvaal, Mr. Gandhi has had unique opportunites of studying the question of passive resistance from its various bearings. In fact, nobody has had such a large experience of the practical working of it as he, and therefore his thoughts and reflections on the subject are worth careful consideration. Briefly they are as follows :—

Only those people whose manhood is highly developed and who are altogether fearless, can become good passive resisters. Women as well as boys and girls who have reached the age of understanding, can also make good passive resisters. It is not necessary that a large number should co-operate in order to keep up the struggle. However, when it is undertaken by a large number, it is likely to be crowned with success much sooner. He says that it can be carried on even by a handful of men or even single-handed, and that if the present fighters were somehow to fall off, he could and would carry it on single-handed. Men who are not endowed with a strong physical constitution can fight the battle as well as those who are physically strong. To make a good passive resister, it is not necessary to exercise the body, or to learn drilling. It is unnecessary for him to know the use of guns and rifles. Even the mighty kings are afraid of those who have acquired mastery over themselves. Their cannon balls and ammunitions of war are powerless to defeat them, and at last they are obliged to yield to their reasonable demands.

ITS DEVELOPMENT.

Who can say after having known the stuff of which the Transvaal passive resisters are made —men who endured prison life more than once—that they are less brave than the military men? Like military men they carry death in the hollow of their hands. Before entering the lists, they give up all the good things of the world and give up even the craving for earthly possessions. Mr. Gandhi gave up his profession and went to jail on three separate occasions. He was prepared and is still prepared to go there, if the Government dare arrest him. He never troubles himself about thoughts of his family—what would happen to his wife and children during his incarceration, who would give them their daily requirements and who would provide them with the necessary funds. These reflections depress him not. It is a notorious fact that he has not laid by anything against a rainy day, having given away whatever he had, towards the Colony at Phoenix, and the maintenance of *Indian Opinion*. None of the considerations which generally weigh with every so-called wordly-wise men, has deterred him from doing his duty to his country and from going to jail whenever he thought that he was better there than outside. Mr. Dawood Mahomed, Mr. Cachalia, and other leaders of their respective communities, have placed duty before everything else, have sacrificed all their material interests, and gone to jail several times. While they were in jail their European creditors—most of the Indian business is financed by them—on failing to induce them to give up the struggle, pressed them for payment of their debts. Under the circumstances in which they were placed, they could not meet their demands. The result of it all was that their businesses were gone. They are now leading the lives of extreme poverty. So far as sacrifices of the worldly possessions go, the passive resisters of the Transvaal have in a number of instances given greater proofs of their having done so than the men who offer themselves for military service.

Women as well as boys and girls have contributed their quota to the struggle in the Transvaal. Mrs. Rambhabai Sodha, the wife of Mr. Sodha, one of the staunchest passive resisters, dared to cross the frontier and was arrested at Volkstrust. She was duly tried and sentenced to imprisonment. She has appealed against the sentence and in the meanwhile she is free. But she will not flinch if the higher Court orders the sentence to be carried out. Some of the women worked as hawkers of fruits and vegetables, to maintain themselves and their children, while their husbands were undergoing the various terms of imprisonment in the Transvaal jails. Directly and indirectly, they gave every encouragement to their husbands to continue the struggle. There are numerous instances given in the annals of Rajputana by Colonel Todd, where Rajput ladies fought side by side with their husbands or gave them every assistance and encouragement to do so. There are some instances mentioned, of husbands returning defeated from the battle-fields, and being unwelcome to their wives. The same is repeated in the Transvaal. Many a wife has willingly let her husband do his duty to his country, and has parted from him most cheerfully, while on his way to the jail. Not a few have concealed their contempt for their husbands hesitating to do their duty or paying the fine instead. The Indian boys and girls in the Transvaal have also contributed their share to the glorious struggle, each in his or her own way.

At times the struggle in the Transvaal has been strengthened by a very large number of passive resisters, gathering round the banner and at other times their ranks have been thinned. Some of them lose their spirits and give up the fight temporarily. But they join it again when they have overcome the weakness of the flesh. Every one of those who attended the mass meeting at Johannesburg already referred to before, has not been able to carry out his vow literally. Some of them who dreaded the ruin consequent on their joining the struggle in person, and who have not been able to brave the wrath of their European creditors, have contributed largely to the funds of the movement. It is this class of men—the merchants—who have supplied the necessary funds to the war chest for three consecutive years.

The passive resisters of the Transvaal are

largely made up of traders and hawkers. They have had no physical culture and learnt no military drill. They have no acquaintance with guns and rifles, and they do not want to know it either. From personal knowledge of some of these valiant fighters, I can say that some of them used to live in fine Bungalows, drive about in splendid ourn-outs, and otherwise live in great ease and comfort. These very men, on hearing the call of duty, were ready to go to jail and suffer all sorts of privations and humiliations. Those who are familiar with this class of men, and know how much trouble they have undergone in jails, cannot help admiring their bravery and power of endurance which, in several cases, surpass those of the military men.

The struggle in the Transvaal would have successfully ended long ago if the whole force that ought to have been brought to aid it, could have been requisitioned. However, it was not possible to do so. Some of the merchants and traders feared total ruin of their business, if they joined the struggle. To continue their business, they were obliged to comply with the requirements of the Law of 1907 and produced their certificates whenever called upon to do so. The Government did its best to win over such men to their side. The result was that the number of passive resisters was never sufficiently large to bring the Government down on their hips. Notwithstanding this they felt themselves almost helpless before the small band of passive resisters. Of course, they are morally and materially backed up by almost the whole Indian community in South Africa.

General Smuts, the other day, paid a tribute to the manner in which the Indians stood together. The trend of the public press has for a long time been towards granting the Indian demands, and some of the papers have advised the Government to accede to them. The *Transvaal Leader*, at one time most hostile towards the Indians, in a leading article published on the 23rd December 1909, wrote as follows:—

> Are the Asiatics to be kept out by means of a Law which, in their view, needlessly humiliates them as a race, or under Governor's regulations which, being applicable to immigrants from all regions, put no special stigma on their own nationality? Are we to brand a particular race which represents an elder, and in some respects higher, civilization than our own, or shall we take powers which will block the entry of immigrants of all races, unless under the conditions, or within the numbers which, as a State, we may deem it necessary to fix? The admission of Mr. Gandhi and his friends yesterday gives hope that the Government see their way at length to adopt the latter course—that of dealing with individuals without dishonoring the race. Such a concession to a people who include some of the first gentlemen, scholars, and soldiers in the world, and whose better classes are represented to us by professional men of the type of Messrs. Gandhi and Royeppen, is a concession which would be honorable both to themselves and the Transvaal Government. It would heal the deeply-wounded feelings of India, and in so doing remove a lot of anxiety from the mind of the Imperial Government.

The white population of the Transvaal has also changed its attitude towards the Indians. The bitterness of feeling that was so rampant against them at one time, is getting less and less; nay, some of them have become very friendly towards them, and advocate their cause as if it was their own. One great good out of the struggle that is patent to any observer, is that the Indians in the Transvaal have learnt to esteem the possession of the sense of self-respect far higher than men in similar situations in India have in dealing with foreigners. In this respect, their brethren in India might follow them with advantage.

One virtue the passive resisters have to possess in abundance and exercise most assiduously, is truthfulness. If the struggle had lacked in this essential qualification, the Transvaal Indians would have succumbed long ere now. The country that has produced men like Harishchandra, Prahlad, Sudhanva, etc., where men devote their leisure hours to hearing and reciting the merits of their illustrious dead; where, according to Col. Sleeman's personal knowledge of the people, acquired during his rambles and his long period of judgeship, men would refuse to tell an untruth even in cases in which their property, liberty and life depended upon telling a lie; where according to Prof. Max Muller, every foreign traveller to India was particularly struck with one characteristic of the people, *viz.*, their truthfulness; and whose people, living thousands of miles away, to-day maintain their truthful habits against tremendous odds; that country would again occupy a place of honor amongst the other countries of the world if the people in general stuck to that virtue, as in times gone by, through thick and thin. The Transvaal struggle is a good augury for the high destiny of this country once more. Not long ago, the *Times of India* said, and very properly too, that "the Indian nation is being hammered out in South Africa."

Another great virtue that the passive resisters have to practise zealously, is fearlessness. To be a true passive resister, it is necessary that he should be able to brave the consequences of his daring conduct, and to submit calmly to the penalties, which, as the world goes at present, might, in the name of law and order, inflict on him. Men who are engrossed in worldly matters, men whose ideas are, in the first place, to get on in life as best as circumstances permit, and men who cannot risk their private interests for the good of the public at large, can never make good passive resisters. Passive resistance means sacrifice, sacrifice of everything which is tempting in this life. It means service of the people at one's own expense. Unless one's altruism is sufficiently developed, he cannot be fearless, and thus he cannot make an efficient passive resister. Bhartrihari in his Niti-Shatak describes a good type of a passive resister when he says :—

निन्दन्तु नीतिनिपुणा यदि.वा स्तुवन्तु
लक्ष्मी समाविशतु गच्छतु वा यथेष्टम् ।
अद्यैव वा मरणमस्तु युगान्तरे वा
न्याय्यात्पथः प्रविचलन्ति पदं न धीराः ॥

Meaning.—"High-souled men whose lives are based upon great ethical principles may be censured or praised, may acquire as much wealth as they desire, or may be reduced to poverty, may meet with death (on account of their straightforward conduct) or may live for a generation longer, but nothing will cause them to turn away from the path of truth and justice."

The passive resisters of the Transvaal have been true to these teachings. They have not looked to their private interests, they have not troubled themselves about the consequent ruin to themselves and their family, and they have not been scared away by the threats of penalties or by the self-imposed troubles of a jail life. Neither praises nor censures of others have made them swerve from the path of religion and duty that they chalked out for themselves. They have absolute faith in the leadership of Mr. Gandhi and echo his views to the effect that to obey an unjust law is contrary to the dictates of religion and humanity. I have had the pleasure of meeting some of them, and they all seemed to be saturated with this notion. They believe in nothing so much as in the voice of their conscience, and yield to no other dictates so readily as to those of the old man within.

Passive resistance is undoubtedly the best weapon to fight with for promoting all national aims and aspirations,. Even the most unjust and arbitrary acts of a Government could be met by this weapon more effectively than any act of violence. The advantages of soul-force against physical force have been well-pictured by Mr. Gandhi in the following words :—

Passive resistance is an all-sided sword; it can be used anyhow; it blesses him who uses it and him against whom it is used without drawing a drop of blood; it produces far-reaching results. It never rusts and cannot be stolen. Competition between passive resisters does not exhaust them. The sword of passive resistance does not require a scabbard and one cannot be forcibly dispossessed of it.

In order to make the passive resistance struggle a success it must be based on a solid rock of truthfulness. No half-truths will avail. The struggle that has not truth as its fundamental basis, is bound to miscarry. Such a struggle is harmful to the strugglers and the country on whose behalf it is carried on.

Another qualification which those who set duty to their country above all considerations and fight hard to make their country substantially better, is that they should take a vow of poverty. All those who have left a permanent mark in history have been more or less selfless. The great Mahatmas, like Mahavir and Buddha, gave up their palaces and kingdoms to wander about first to learn truth, and then to teach it to others. Thousands of great souls have followed their example since, and even to-day it would not be difficult to come across men, who are found to have given up all earthly possessions with a view to work single-mindedly for the elevation of the souls of others. Even in these materialistic days, one comes across selfless *Sanyasins* who gladly bear the badge of poverty. The amount of self-sacrifice that the Indians are capable of displaying in a great cause, and the degree of cheerfulness and readiness with which they can bear privations can hardly be equalled in the history of any other people. The one great factor that inspires men to be contented and happy, though their earthly possessions are almost nil, is that they have very few wants, and they are such as can be supplied with the smallest possible effort. Of late, the Indians have begun to allow themselves greater latitude in this respect than in former times, by aping the manners and customs of the Europeans. They are actuated by the same materialistic tendencies which are so rampant in Europe. Fortunately, however, for India, their number is not very large. If the people of India were to adopt the costly ways and manners of Europe and their costly institutions, they would be grossly steeped in materialism regardless of the teachings of their forefathers. The result would be that the people would not be able to keep up the high religious and moral tone that they have maintained hitherto, and that they would begin to degenerate in every way. Mr. Gandhi and his colleagues who have chosen to lead lives of poverty, all for the sake of their country, have, in so doing, merely followed the teachings of the Indian sages of old. The good of the country depends a great deal upon the amount of selfless work done by its sons and the larger the number of such men in the country, the greater will be the resulting good to its people. Mr. Gandhi believes that those alone can render great service to the people who take to simple life, as in ages past, can rest contented with simple and coarse fare and lead lives of simplicity. Yielding to the weakness of the flesh in the matter of diet, drinks, etc., makes one effeminate, particularly so in the hot climate of India. As regards work, he advocates greater resort to hand labour, and particularly to hand weaving, and depreciates services of all sorts. He thinks the latter quite as demoralising as the worship of modern materialism.

In addition to the three attributes, *viz.*, Truthfulness, Fearlessnes, and Poverty, as essential requisites for the service of one's Motherland, Mr. Gandhi advocates a fourth, that is, celibacy. He says that so far as the power of control over all human passions and desires goes, none can exercise it better than he who practises celibacy. India is a country of real live Brahmacharies. They are to be found everywhere. Some take to it from their youth, and some after having been householders for a few years. A real Brahmachari invariably possesses the other three attributes, and has hardly to be taught to cultivate them. By virtue of the position he has taken up, he is poor and fearless, and there is no reason why he should not prize truth at its real valuation. Such men alone can make ideal passive resisters.

Mr. Gandhi acts up to the above principles and inculcates them to those who come in contact with him. His son Harilal is trying to follow his father to the best of his ability and has been to jail several times as a passive resister. He is not supposed to have any legal right to enter the Transvaal, though his father has. His second son Manilal, who is now about 17, seems to be a chip of the same old block. He entered the Transvaal and took to hawking. He was arrested and sentenced more than once for hawking without a license. When not in jail, he leads as simple a life as his father, and the report goes that he is going to be a perfect Brahmachari. The example that Mr. Gandhi sets, is indeed contagious. In the issue of the *Indian Opinion* of the 29th January, 1910, it is reported that Mr. Royeppen, B. A., of the Cambridge University, a Barrister-at-Law, and a Christian by birth, was arrested—while hawking without a license, that he has given up the intention of getting enrolled in any of the Courts of South Africa and practising there as a Barrister, and that he has made up his mind to lead a life of poverty and to serve his mother-country.

THE SIMPLICITY OF LIFE.

It will not be out of place to mention here the sort of life that Mr. Gandhi usually leads in South Africa. His life is really very simple, and he manages to live on 15 rupees a month in the Transvaal where everything is expensive. He prefers country life to city life. He has a positive dislike for city life on account of its environments and its vices. In such a cold climate as that of Johannesburg, he takes two purely vegetarian meals, and takes no other beverage than pure water or milk. He usually takes his first meal at about one or half-past one in the afternoon. It consists mostly of fruits and nuts. The second meal comes off at about seven in the evening, and as a rule it is of his own cooking. He has given up taking tea, coffee, cocoa, etc., as these articles are mostly prepared with the help of indentured labour. He generally performs his own domestic services, such as cleaning cooking utensils, sweeping the house, making up his bed, etc. In these matters also he acts on the principle of equality for all and would not allow any one to render him such services as could be rendered for him by himself. His dietary is very simple as a rule, consisting only of bread, vegetables and fruits, and he never allows himself anything that is not absolutely required for health. In his younger days, he made various experiments on his person to find out the bare minimum required to keep his body and soul together, and ultimately he has hit upon this dietary. He believes that by meeting the bare necessities of life, the soul is better purified. Writing to me lately from the Tolstoy Farm, where he is now living with a number of passive resisters' families, he says :—

> I prepare the bread that is required on the farm. The general opinion about it is that it is well made. Manilal and a few others have learnt how to prepare it. We put in no yeast and no baking powder. We grind our own wheat. We have just prepared some marmalade from the oranges grown on the farm. I have also learnt how to prepare ceramel coffee. It can be given as a beverage even to babies. The passive resisters on the farm have given up the use of tea and coffee, and taken to ceramel coffee prepared on the farm. It is made from wheat which is first baked in a certain way and then ground. We intend to sell our surplus production of the above three articles to the public later on. Just at present, we are working as labourers on the construction work that is going on, on the farm, and have not time to produce more of the articles above mentioned than we need for ourselves.

In the bitterest cold, he bathes in cold water and sleeps in the open verandah. When he goes out, he is obliged to dress in European style, but at home his dress is mostly of Indian style. When he was last in India, he used to dress mostly in pure Indian style, wearing clothes made by hand. While practising as a Barrister in Kathiawar, he used to appear in the local Courts in his Indian costume, with Indian-made sandals to his feet; and according to *the time immemorial* custom in India, would leave his sandals outside the Court before presenting himself to the Judge. He has, in fact, gone through such a long course of training in the methods of living a life according to nature, that to do so has become quite a second nature with him now. That is how life in the Transvaal jails was by no means irksome to him. On the contrary, he considered it a blessing to be in jail, when his duty to his country demanded it of him.

What a vast change there is in his present life, and that of twelve years ago, when I put up with him, as his guest in his house situated not far from the Durban beach! The late Mr. Escombe, for a long time Attorney-General of Natal, was almost his next-door neighbour. Even then, so far as he himself was concerned, his life was simple enough; but now it is much nearer the natural life than ever. Like the Yogi of Bhartrihari as depicted in the following Shloka, he is quite as happy—perhaps happier—now as he was in those days. The Shloka in the Nitishataka is:—

क्वचिद्भूमौ शायी क्वचिदपि च पर्यङ्क शयनः
क्वचिच्छाकाहारी क्वचिदपि च शाल्योदन रुचिः ।
क्वचित् कंथाधारी क्वचिदपि च दिव्याम्बरधरो
मनस्वी कार्यार्थी न गणयति दुःखम् न च सुखम् ॥

Meaning.—"A benevolently disposed person who is simply anxious only to do his duty on some occasions sleeps on the bare ground, and on others, on finely-made beds and beddings; on some occasions he lives on mere fruits and roots, and on others, on nicely prepared dishes; on some occasions, he wraps himself up in a tattered quilt, and on others, he is finely dressed; living under such opposite conditions of life, such a man is equally happy, whether it is one or the other."

Mr. Doke in his book writes that what Kipling has written about Poorandas, is equally applicable in the case of Mr. Gandhi. He says, "This is a graphic picture of our friend." The ascetic of Bhartrihari, the Poorandas of Kipling and the Gandhi of Mr. Doke seem to be formed of the same metal, and I am not sure that the latter would allow the imaginary characters of Bhartrihari and Kipling to outdistance him in the race, if such was possible.

LIFE IN JAIL.

When Mr. Gandhi was sentenced by the presiding Magistrate at Volkstrust to two months' rigorous imprisonment, or as he himself put it in a note to Mr. Doke, "to partake of the hospitality of King Edward's hotel," for failing to produce his certificate of Registration and for refusing to give thumb and finger impressions for the sake of identification, as if such identification was at all necessary in his case—he wrote in the same chit saying of himself "the happiest man in the Transvaal." He has published what the nature of the happiness was that he has had in the Transvaal jails and what his experiences were on three different occasions, in the form of small brochures. I shall here give a few extracts from them to show what an unenviable life he had while there. Those who wish to be more enlightened as to the power of self-control and self-renunciation that Mr. Gandhi is capable of bringing to bear on his life and work, would do well to go through the original, published by the International Press, Phoenix, Natal.

Each and every person who is sentenced by any competent Court to imprisonment in the Transvaal jail, independent of the nature of the offence committed by him, is obliged to wear prison clothes. The dresses worn and the blankets used by any one prisoner are given to any other. They are not always sufficiently clean. Those sentenced to hard labour are made to work for 9 hours a day. They are sometimes employed in road repairing, sometimes in breaking metal, sometimes in doing earthwork, *viz.*, digging and carrying earth from one place to another, and occasionally in gardening and such other work. Mr. Gandhi writes as follows in his book No. 2 on jail experiences:—

Every prisoner in the jail on getting up in the morning is required to fold his own bedding, and to place it in its proper place. He must finish his toilet by 6 o'clock and be ready to start out at the stroke of the hour. The work begins at 7 o'clock. It is of various kinds. On the first day, we were taken to an open place, not far from the main road, to dig it so as to convert it into arable land. About thirty Indians were taken to this place. None of those who could not carry out this work, was obliged to go there. We were taken along with the Kaffirs. The ground to be dug was very hard. It was to be worked upon with spades, and hence the work proved too hard. Again, it was a very hot day. The place we were taken to was about a mile and a half from the jail. Each one of us started very well indeed. But as none of us was used to this kind of work, it was not long before we were quite done up. As the day advanced the work seemed harder still. The warder was very strict. He used to cry out every now and then "go on, go on." This made the Indians quite nervous. I saw some of them weeping. One of them had a swollen foot. All this caused me a great deal of heart-burning, and yet on every occasion, I reminded them of the duty, and asked them to perform it as well as possible, with a good heart, and without minding the words of the warder. I felt myself done up also. My hands were covered with blisters and water was oozing out of them. I could hardly bend the spade and felt the weight of it as if it was quite a maund. I prayed to God to preserve my honour, to maintain my limbs intact, and to bestow on me sufficient strength to be able to perform my allotted task. I trusted to Him and went on with my work. The warder would sometimes remonstrate with me at an occasional break required to get over the fatigue. I told him that it was unnecessary for him to remind me of my duty, and that I was prepared to go through as much of it as was possible for me to do. Just then I saw Mr. Jhinabhai faint......... While I was pouring water on Jhinabhai's head, the following occurred to me. 'Most of the Indians trusted my word, and submitted themselves to imprisonment. If the advice that I happened to offer them were erroneous how much sin I would be committing in the eyes of God in tendering it to them. They underwent all sorts of hardships on account of that advice. With this thought in my mind, I heaved a deep sigh.' With God as my witness, I reflected on the subject once more, and was immediately reassured that it was all right. I felt that the advice that I tendered to them was the only advice that I could under the circumstances. In anticipation of future happiness, it was absolutely necessary that we should undergo the hardest trials and sufferings in the first instance, and that there was no reason to be grieved at the latter. This was simply a fit of fainting, but even if it was a case of death how could I offer any other advice than what I had already done ? It at once occurred to me that it was more honourable for anybody to die suffering in that manner, than to continue living a life of perpetual enslavement. With this thought I recovered my usual spirits, and asked Jhinabhai to keep up his .... The prisoners are allowed one hour for their meals between 12 and 1 o'clock, and are obliged to work again from 1 to 5 o'clock.

In the jail, the prisoners have to sweep their own cells, to clear out their own piss-pots, and to clean the water-closets. With reference to the latter, Mr. Gandhi writes thus :

At one time one of the warders came to me, and asked me to provide him with two of his men to clean the water-closets. I thought that I could do nothing better than clean them myself, and so I offered him my services. I have no particular dislike to that kind of work. On the contrary, I am of opinion that we ought to get ourselves accustomed to it.

At times prisoners are transferred from one jail to another. On those occasions they are brought out in their prison garb, and made to carry their belongings themselves from the jail to the neighbouring railway station, and from the station to the other jail. In this way, Mr. Gandhi used to be transferred from one jail to another, and was made to travel in the third class. While being thus taken, he used to be handcuffed also. This created great commotion at the time.

Sometimes they are made to sleep in cells occupied by dangerous and vicious persons. Referring to this, Mr. Ghandi says :—

I was given a bed in a ward, where there were principally Kaffiir patients. Here I passed the whole night in great misery and terror. I did not know then that I was to be taken the next day to another cell that was occupied by Indian prisoners. Fretting that I would be kept incarcerated with such men, I got very nervous and terror-stricken. And yet I tried my best to reconcile myself to the idea that it was my duty to undergo the sufferings that may befall me. I read from the Bhagawad-Gita, that I had with me, certain verses suited to the occasion, and on pondering over them, was soon reconciled to the situation. The chief reason why I got nervous was that in the same room, there were a number of wild, murderous-looking, vicious Kaffir and Chinese prisoners. I did not know their language. One of the Kaffirs began to ply me with all sorts of questions. As far as I could gather, he seemed to be mocking me indecently. I did not understand what his questions were, and I kept quiet. He then asked me in his broken English, "Why have they brought you here?". I gave him a very short reply and was again silent. He was followed by one of the Chinamen. He was worse than the other. He approached my bed, and looked at me intently. I kept on my silence. He then proceeded towards the above-mentioned Kaffir's bed. There they began to mock each other indecently, and expose their private parts. Both these prisoners were probably there for murder or highway robbery. How could I enjoy sleep after seeing these dreadful things?

According to Jail rules the water-closets in the jails must be kept unfastened even when a prisoner is in. He is allowed to remain in only a short time to answer the call of nature. While Mr. Gandhi was in jail, he has had a very hard time of it in this particular matter. He says:—

(At one time) as soon as I got seated there to answer the call of nature, a very wild and muscular looking Kaffir turned up. He asked me to get off from the seat, and began to abuse me. I told him I would not be long when he took hold of me, and threw me outside. Fortunately, I was able to catch hold of one of the doors, and to save myself from a nasty fall. This did not make me very nervous. I simply walked away with a smiling countenance. But one or two Indian prisoners who happened to see the situation in which I was placed, could not restrain themselves from shedding tears.

The worst of the jail life is want of sufficient and nutritious food. The jail diet principally consists of Indian corn and dry beans. Our people are not used to the dietary on which the Kaffirs can thrive. The short-term prisoners—and the passive resisters are invariably short-term prisoners—are not allowed any ghee, and both the Hindus and the Mahomedans refuse to take what is offered instead, *viz.*, lard, because its use is forbidden by their religion. They all had to be satisfied with a semi-starvation dietary. In this matter Mr. Gandhi suffered great hardships during his third term of imprisonment of three months in the Pretoria jail. He writes :—

"My diet consisted of broth made of Indian corn every morning, the same kind of broth with potatoes or carrots thrice a week, and beans for the other three days, at noon, and rice without ghee in the evening. The mid-day meal on Wednesday consisted of beans, rice and ghee, and on Sundays of rice and ghee. It is hardly possible to eat rice without ghee, and so I determined not to eat rice until ghee was supplied along with it. The broth given in the morning as well as at mid-day was sometimes watery, and sometimes half-boiled. The beans were at times half cooked also, but usually they were well done. When vegetables were allowed, they consisted either of four small potatoes or only three small carrots, which counted as 8 ozs. In the morning sometimes, I would take four or five spoonfuls of broth, but as a rule I lived simply upon what was allowed to me at mid-day according to rules, and that was my only meal."

Mr. Gandhi begged of the medical man in charge to allow ghee instead of lard to all the Indian prisoners. The gentleman offered it to him alone. But he made up his mind not to avail himself of the offer, until the other prisoners were allowed the same. He says :—

"The very same day bread and rice were placed before me. I was really very hungry, but how could I take bread like that, as a passive resister? And I refused to take either." In the meanwhile, he continued nagging at the matter. In this way a month and a half passed away, when an order was received to the effect that in those jails where there was a large number of Indian passive resisters, ghee was to be served. He writes : "After struggling in this matter for a month and a half I was relieved from the pangs of a self-imposed semi-starvation diet."

DUTY BEFORE ANYTHING ELSE.

While reading the above account of the sufferings undergone by the passive resisters in the Transvaal jails, the readers will have drawn their own conclusions of their character, each in his own different way. Some will ask why Indians in the Transvaal allow themselves to be put to so many sufferings, why they prefer to be arrested and sent to jails where they are obliged to perform the most dirty work—such as they have been prohibited by their religion to do. Others will ask why instead of remaining in such an inhospitable land, they do not return to their mother-country, and why they hanker for a big loaf, when that can probably be secured only after such terrible sufferings. It is better to remain satisfied with only a small loaf, which can always be secured—and that without much difficulty—by any willing worker in his own land. A number of men put to me questions of the kind while I was engaged in collecting funds for the passive resisters. With regard to such questions, Mr. Gandhi has expressed himself as follows. His views deserve a very careful perusal and consideration :

The one view is why one should go to jail and there submit himself to all personal restraints, a place where he would have to dress himself in the coarse and ugly prison garb of a felon and to live upon non-nutritious and semi-starvation diet, where he is sometimes kicked about by jail officials, and made to do every kind of work whether he liked it or not, where he has to carry out the behests of a warder who is no better than his household servant, where he is not allowed to receive the visits of his friends and relatives and is prohibited from writing to them, where he is denied almost the bare necessities of life and is sometimes obliged to sleep in the same cell that is occupied by actual thieves and robbers. The question is why one should undergo such trials and sufferings. Better is death than life under such conditions. Far better to pay up the fine than to be thus incarcerated. May God spare his creatures from such sufferings in jail. Such thoughts make one really a coward, and being in constant dread of a jail life, deter him from undertaking to perform services in the interests of his country which might otherwise prove very valuable.

The other view is that it would be the height of one's good fortune to be in jail in the interests and good name of one's country and religion. There, there is very little of that misery which he has usually to undergo in daily life. There, he has to carry out the orders of one warder only, whereas in daily life he is obliged to carry out the behests of a great many more. In the jail, he has no anxiety to earn his daily bread and to prepare his meals. The Government sees to all that. It also looks after his health for which he has to pay nothing. He gets enough work to exercise his body. He is freed from all his vicious habits. His soul is thus free. He has plenty of time at his disposal to pray to God. His body is restrained, but not his soul. He learns to be more regular in his habits. Those who keep his body in restraint, look after it. Taking this view of jail life, he feels himself quite a free being. If any misfortune comes to him or any wicked warder happens to use any violence towards him, he learns to appreciate and exercise patience, and is pleased to have an opportunity of keeping control over himself. Those who think this way are sure to be convinced that even jail life can be attended with blessings. It solely rests with individuals and their mental attitude to make it one of blessing or otherwise. I trust, however, that the readers of this my second experience of life in the Transvaal jail will be convinced that the real road to ultimate happiness lies in going to jail and undergoing sufferings and privations there in the interests of one's country and religion.

Placed in a similar position for refusing his poll tax, the American citizen, Thoreau, expressed similar thoughts in 1849. Seeing the walls of the cell in which he was confined, made of solid stone two or three feet thick, and the door of wood and iron a foot thick, he said to himself thus:—

"I saw that, if there was a wall of stone between me and my townsmen, there was a still more difficult one to climb or break through before they could get to be as free as I was. I did not feel for a moment confined, and the walls seemed a great waste of stone and mortar. I felt as if I alone of all my townsmen had paid my tax. They plainly did not know how to treat me, but behaved like persons who are underbred. In every threat and in every compliment there was a blunder; for they thought that my chief desire was to stand the other side of the stone-wall. I could not but smile to see how industriously they locked the door on my meditations, which followed them out again without let or hindrance, and they were nearly all that was dangerous. As they could not reach me, they had resolved to punish my body; just as boys if they cannot come to some person against whom they have a spite, will abuse his dog. I saw that the State was half-witted, that it was timid as a lone woman with her silver spoons, and that it did not know its friends from its foes, and I lost all my remaining respect for it, and pitied it."

An ordinary man would have been cowed down by the troubles and sufferings of the kind that Mr. Gandhi went through in the Transvaal jails, but in his case, they have made him the more determined in his aims and aspirations from the national point of view. He is always willing and ready to go through any amount of suffering for the sake of principles and in the interests of his country. Those who have come in contact with him are lately convinced that no self-sacrifice would be too much for him where the honour of his country was concerned and that he was living simply for the cause he had made his own. Before he made his first acquaintance with the Transvaal jails, his time was more or less divided between legal work and public business, and it could hardly be called his own. He was for a long time seeking for some leisure to be able to ponder over the problems of life, but he could not get it anywhere until he was sent to jail, and he was heartily glad to have it even in such an unearthly place as that.

No sooner was he out of it than he began to pour forth the result of that study and deep meditation, and the pages of the *Indian Opinion* from that day contain very interesting reflections on some of the problems of the day. He placed some of his thoughts thereon before large and important gatherings in London during his stay there. Let us here try to give a short summary of the conclusions to which he had by that time arrived with regard to some of the Indian problems.

THE HIGH IDEALS OF THE ANCIENT HINDUS.

He believes that the ancient civilisation of India is far superior to any other, and the main ground for that conclusion is that it is based on religion and high ethical principles. He says that in no other civilisation, religion and morality form such important factors as in that of the Indian civilisation, and therefore has a high reverence for it as well as for the country which gave birth to it. The fervour of his patriotism is of such a high order that he would not take a single step before measuring its full consequences, and would never jeopardise the vital interests of his country, however much he may be goaded to swerve from the high path he has chalked out for himself towards performing his duty to it. The readers of Mr. Doke's book in which several instances of personal assault are related, must have been surprised at the amount of self-control that he possesses even under the gravest provocation. Some of the assaults were certainly highly criminal, and if he had resorted to legal remedies or retaliation, no one could have taken exception to them. But he would not and could not entertain such a thought. It is the love of his country that took him to jail on three different occasions. He asks if this country were a partner in the British Empire, as almost everybody believes and makes others believe, how is it that that partner of the Empire has no voice whatever in the management thereof, and how can the Transvaal, which is another partner therein, prohibit British Indians from entering the country? According to the British Constitution and the Proclamation of 1858, the Indians stand, as naturally also, they do on a footing of equality with the rest of the British subjects in the Empire. He says that he has no objection to continue to remain one of the subjects in the Empire conducted on those lines. In one of his addresses delivered in London in the year 1909, he declared to the effect that he was content to remain the subject of an Empire in which he had only one per cent. share, but that if he had to remain there simply as a slave, the Empire had no meaning whatever for him. The Asiatic Immigration Restriction laws of the Transvaal cut at this very principle of the Empire, and put an unnecessary stigma on the good name of India. He could not bear to see his country dishonoured and discredited anywhere, because of the colour its people wore, or the creed they followed; and therefore he thought it his bounden duty to protest against the differential laws of the Transvaal in the only way that was open to him. He considers patriotism a part of his religion. No self-sacrifice is too much for him when the interests of his country are involved. He says that in the country in which Religion and Ethics are at a discount, there patriotism suffers, but that where people are guided by religion and high principles of morality, there they stand on a far higher level of manhood. He preaches to his followers not to swerve from the high ideals of the ancient Hindus, and says that if they did so, self-government would be theirs before long. He has been trying to bring home to everybody his idea, that the civilization of ancient India is of such a high order that Indians have little need to learn anything from any other civilisation, but that the other nations have plenty to learn, if they choose, from Indians. Vegetarianism, teetotalism, personal cleanliness, and the various social institutions on which Indian society is based, are being appreciated the more and more since Europe and Asia have been thrown so much together. During the last 25 years the progress made in the city of London on the lines inculcated by the Indian sages thousands of years ago, has been very great indeed. To-day, one comes across Vegetarian Restaurants there in almost every important centre, where, contrary to their custom, no alcoholic drinks are ever supplied. The number of men frequenting these is always on the increase. Curdled milk and what with bread make the staple diet of the Indians all over the Continent. Their great medicinal virtues are known to everybody in India. But in Europe, nobody thought of them till Dr. Metchnicoff, of Paris, the winner of the Nobel Prize in Medicine a couple of years ago, advocated their great health-giving properties, and now a lot of people in London and Paris use them daily, as a natural key-to health and long life. Dr. Metchnicoff himself takes a bowl of curdled milk every day, finding that it keeps him in a remarkable state of health. Eastern thoughts are often garbed in Western language and sent out again as brand-new discoveries for the good of humanity in general. As a rule, the houses of the middle class people and those still lower in the social scale in Europe have hardly any baths in their houses. To them bathing was quite a luxury and very few could afford the means for it. But the putting up of public baths at convenient distances by the London County Council, and the number of those resorting to them, testifies to the rapid advance made by public opinion, towards personal cleanliness and particularly with reference to that of the humbler classes in the metropolis of the world.

There are a great many thinkers who see the national folly of trying to live too richly. These men are doing their best to inculcate ideas of simple life, including simple but healthy and nutritious vegetarian diet. There are a number of societies formed in England for the promotion of these objects. A society called "the New Crusade" has been started with the object of promoting simple life as well as handicrafts. Those who became members of the body, try to live according to the ideals set by it. Last year I visited the hand-loom factory at Haslemere near London under Mr. Godfrey Blount (he has written a number of books on simple life) when I was told that there was a very large demand for the fabrics made there, and that they were not able to cope with that large demand. Cottage Industries, once the pride of India, are being strongly advocated by this Society. The advocates of Cottage Industries would like to displace power-looms by hand-looms. In social and religious matters also, India can teach a lot to others. The system of cremation, which is purely a Hindu institution, founded thousands of years ago, is being appreciated by the thinking population of Europe, and at the present day the number of the dead sent to the Paris and Woking (near London) Crematoria is not inconsiderable. In fact, questions pertaining to life and living have been solved once for all by our ancestors thousands of years ago. It is with reference to the teachings on such questions that the late Prof. Max Muller in his book "India: What can it teach us?", compliments the Indian sages of old. At page 6 of the book he says :—

> If I were to look over the whole world to find out the country most richly endowed with all the wealth, power, and beauty that Nature can bestow—in some parts the very paradise on this earth—I should point to India. If I were asked under what sky the human mind has most fully developed some of its choicest gifts, has most deeply pondered on the greatest problems of life, and has found solutions of some of them which well deserve the attention even of those who have studied Plato and Kant—I should point to India. And if I were to ask myself from what literature we, here in Europe, we who have been nurtured almost exclusively on the thoughts of Greeks and Romans, and of one Semetic race, the Jewish, may draw that corrective which is most wanted in order to make our inner life more perfect, more comprehensive, more universal, in fact, more truly human, a life, not for this life only, but a transfigured and eternal life—again I should point to India.

The basic principles of the Indian civilization are self-sacrifice, self-control and self-renunciation. It inculcates the good of humanity at large and teaches its votaries to give up egoism and to work for the communal good. Unlike other civilizations, it enjoins fasts and penances in order that the body may be inured to suffering and privations. Modern civilization, however, inculcates progress of man on different lines. To obtain the means, whereby ease, comfort and plenty could be secured during one's existence, no matter how much it may cost others, is the principal aim of individuals as well as of nations. The main policy of each of the European nations is to seek its own aggrandisement at the expense of the other and to adopt the most effective means to check the other's aggrandisement. That is the reason why the European nations have to maintain to-day such huge armies and navies at enormous costs, the burden of which is becoming heavier and heavier from year to year, and against which the groanings of the people are now becoming more and more audible. The more they look upon each other with jealous eyes, the more their burden increases. In India, the teaching has been quite the reverse. There, men are taught to control all their passions and desires which are looked upon as the chief enemies men need fear, and to live a simple, healthy and unencumbered life. Mr. Gandhi believes that the more we divorce ourselves from the practice of the high virtues enjoined by our scriptures, the greater will be our downward march, that the more we look to individual interests, the greater will be the loss of our community, and that the more we seek for material riches, the greater will be the poverty of the nation. The basis of Indian civilisation and Indian culture, being the good of humanity at large, even at the sacrifice of our own individual good, our spirits inwardly revolt at our occasional puny attempts to emulate other nations towards the achievement of riches and material comforts. The result in most cases is that we are placed in a sorry plight, and are neither here, there, nor anywhere.

SOME MODERN TENDENCIES.

At the present day, the people of Europe are vieing with each other in increasing the means that conduce to bodily comforts, and in aping the lives of men in better material circumstances. The old indigenous populations of America and Australia are by now almost extinct, and their places are taken up by people from every part of Europe. Africa is partitioned by the different nations of Europe, each of which has large spheres of influences therein, and each of which is busy in exploiting its vast resources to the detriment of the aboriginal population. The aim and object of the immigrants of all classes is to live well, as well as their neighbours, whether they can or not, and then they cannot always afford to be particular as to the means of obtaining the wherewithal to do so. The original sons of the soil are ignored altogether, and treated as so many hewers of wood and drawers of water for their so-called betters. This state of things is well illustrated in a number of books that have been written on the atrocities perpetrated on the people of the Congo under the late King Leopald's regime, at the instance of a handful of capitalists, financiers and stock-jobbers with the result that the aborigines are being crushed out of existence. The whole of the Congo Basin was declared the private property of King Leopald, and the people were allowed only such pieces of land as were actually under occupation by them. By a stroke of the pen, King Lecpald and ultimately the Belgian State became the virtual owner of all the land and its products. The principal attraction of this fertile soil is its vast forests of rubber trees growing there for centuries past. The people are forced to collect all the rubber for the benefit of the State alone, and for such collection, they have to put in the majority of cases the labour of from 20 to 25 days in a month. If any one converts any part of it to his own use, he is considered guilty of theft or of receiving stolen property. In this way, some of the companies are able to declare annual dividends of from 300 to 700 per cent. By the treaty of Berlin of 1885, all the principal powers of Europe bound themselves in the name of the Almighty God to watch over its enforcement. Its sixth clause was:

> All the Powers exercising sovereign rights or influence in these territories pledged themselves to watch over the preservation of the native populations and the improvement of their moral and material conditions of existence, and to work together for the suppression of slavery and the slave trade.

In writing as to how the united nations of Europe kept this pledge, Sir Arthur Conan

Doyle in his book: "The Crime of the Congo" says as follows :—

It is a disgrace to each of them, including ourselves, the way in which they have fulfilled that oath. Before their eyes as I shall show in the sequel, they have had enacted one long horrible tragedy, vouched for by priests and missionaries, traders, travellers and consuls, all corroborated by a Belgian Commission of inquiry. They have seen these unhappy people, who were their wards, robbed of all they possessed, debauched, degraded, mutilated, tortured, murdered, all on such a scale as has never, to my knowledge, occurred before in the whole course of history, and now after all these years, with the facts notorious, we are still at the stage of polite diplomatic expostulations.

After describing how the aborigines were dispossessed of all their lands and all the produce thereof, and how they were enforced to give their labour of 20 to 25 days every month for the sole benefit of the new state, and after deprecating the new form of slavery, much worse than the slavery recognised in old times, introduced as a result of the modern ideas of progress, he says that human nature is almost the same everywhere, and summarises his conclusions in the following terms :—

The fact is that the running of a tropical colony is of all tests, the most searching as to the development of the nation which attempts it; to see helpless people and not to oppress them, to see great wealth and not to confiscate it, to have absolute power and not to abuse it, to raise the native instead of sinking yourself, these are the supreme trials of a nation's spirit. We have all failed at times. But never has there been failure so hopeless, so shocking, bearing such consequences to the world, such degradation to the good name of Christianity and civilization as the failure of the Belgians in the Congo.

The people of Europe and America are being divided into two distinct and separate classes, the rich and the poor, or the capitalists and the labourers. Day by day, the rich are getting richer and the poor poorer. The rich are daily multiplying all sorts of mechanical appliances and labour-saving apparatuses, and the skilled and the unskilled workmen are being brought within the fold of common labourers working as mere tools of those machines. When in the Northern States of America, a few individuals had amassed fabulous sums of money, it was easy for them to obtain free labour and particularly white, *i. e.*, more skilled labour, and they helped to bring about the emancipation of the African Negroes from slavery. Such slavery being no more required under the altered circumstances of society, the Northern States coerced the Southern States to follow their example, and had it abolished from the South at the point of the bayonet. The richer a man is, the greater is his capacity for controlling the lives of a large number of men whom he is in a position to reduce ultimately to the condition of mere slaves, and whom, as a matter of fact, he usually reduces to that condition. These men often regard wealth as everything and men nothing. The American multi-millionaire, Mr. Piermont Morgan, is reported to be managing business and industrial concerns of an aggregate capital of five hundred million pounds, and yet according to Taylor eight millions of men in the United States are badly fed, badly clothed and badly housed. Likewise although the annual income of the people of the British Isles is computed to be eighteen hundred millions sterling, there are a million and a half of women working in factories and mines, from morning till evening, from the age of 14 till they die, in order to eke out their daily pittance. The filthy atmosphere, in which they have to live, curtails life, and their life-long environments are such as to preclude the development of those womanly qualities which are their birthright. With the growth of factories in number and dimensions, and the further introduction of labour-saving appliances, the number of the unemployed also grows, and those of them that are able to find employment, are not always able to earn enough to provide themselves and their family with even the bare means of subsistence. Although the factory hands obtained more wages in these days, their social happiness is very much less than that of men engaged in agriculture and similar pursuits.

The growth of wealth amongst nations as amongst individuals is not at all conducive to the development of the higher virtues of man. The rich as a rule yield to all sorts of temptations that are thrown in their way, and give themselves up to the pleasures of life. The men that are brought up in luxury lose in course of time, all virility, and their sense of justice and morality gets quite benumbed. A lot of their time is taken up in adorning their persons and in attending to social calls and vapid amusements, and ultimately they are so estranged from the other classes that they get quite callous to their wrongs, some of which are of their own making. In the countries of Europe, a number of factories have been set up for the preparation of mercury and lead, sulphur and phosphorus,chlorine gas and bleaching powder, acids and alkalies, and various other chemical preparations of a similar nature. Some of them are poisonous to the touch, and on being absorbed through the skin produce their mischievous effects on the system. The gases that are set free during the manufacture of the various compounds out of them, are so deleterious to health, that the workers thereof have their constitutions undermined before they are long in it, and some of them, if inhaled in large doses, prove instantaneously fatal. A large number of these workers have swollen gums, loose teeth, sallow and anæmic complexions and various other effects of blood poisoning. Some of them are hardly able to masticate their food and are obliged to pass their lives on slops and beer. These gases act on vegetable life still more powerfully. For miles around some of these factories, there is hardly any vegetation, not even a blade of grass is to be seen. And yet the factory owners are not deterred from going on with their manufactures. On the contrary, whenever there is a glut in the market, as generally happens every two or three years in every business, they either shut up the factories and turn the men out in the streets, or offer them very much lower wages, which they are often obliged to accept on account of their inability to procure any other employment in the meanwhile. The present-day industrialism has bred selfishness and greed amongst those engaged in them on an unparalleled scale. Men are so much taken up in feeding and financing the gigantic concerns, and in trying to obtain large dividends for the capital they have invested therein, that they have no leisure left for devoting their time for the good of others, much less for the cause of the poor and the down-trodden. No doubt, some of their Parliaments try to remedy the evils when they become patent enough, but even then factory owners know how to drive a coach-and-four through some of them.

The principal end and aim of individuals under modern conditions is to acquire riches and spend them on objects that gratify their individual selves. Even the definition of civilization in modern times has undergone complete metamorphosis. Now-a-days that man is considered "civilised" who manages anyhow to live in a fine house, to dress well, to command sumptuous meals, to drink high-class wines and spirits, and who devotes his time towards procuring the means for living that sort of high life. Most of the houses of the so-called civilised men are elegantly furnished, having the best cushioned chairs and satin, finest carpets, most costly pictures, etc. They have electric bells in every part of the house to call their servants, and have electric installations for lighting and ventilating them. Almost every article that conduces to ease and comfort is there. The bedrooms are furnished with handsome bedsteads and fine feather-beds and pillows, with washing and dressing tables and most elegant-looking wardrobes. The windows are covered with curtains and blinds for ornamentation or for preventing light penetrating therein and disturbing the owner's sleep. Objects of art, pleasing and captivating to the eye, are to be met with at every step. In winter, the houses are warmed with electricity or steam pipes, and in summer they are cooled by cooling apparatus, so that one uniform temperature may be maintained therein the whole year round. From the time they get out of bed until they get in there again, they arrange to have something to eat every three or four hours, with tea, coffee, alcoholic drinks, etc., in the intervals. They spend their leisure hours in music and concerts, in dancing and story-telling or in card-playing and sports. One charge laid against the Indians in South Africa is that they do not live in finely furnished houses, they do not sleep on soft feather beds, they do not dress according to the European fashion, they do not arrange to eat every three or four hours, most of them do not allow a single drop of liquor to enter their premises, they use tea, coffee, tobacco, etc., very sparingly, and do not spend their leisure hours in theatres and music halls and card-playing. The very life that the Indians are taught by their wise ancestors to lead, and which is at the present day recommended to the Europeans by their thinkers as the most proper life for decent people to lead, is held by the majority of the white settlers in South Africa as a ground for persecuting them. Their very virtues are tabooed, and made a ground for hunting them out of the country.

The other great indications of modern civilization are railways, steamers, automobiles, air-ships, aeroplanes, telegraphs, telephones, gramophones, etc. The mechanical appliances are being multiplied and new inventions introduced almost from day to day. What is good to-day, becomes too antique to-morrow. The quick and cheap travelling by rail at 50 to 60 miles and by steamships at 15 to 25 knots per hour, has completely revolutionised modern society. The automobiles are completing the work begun by railways. They can go even faster than the latter, sometimes at the rate of 80 miles an hour, if the road is well constructed. Even the most secluded country spots of the old times are beginning to be frequented like highway thoroughfares. The greater the speed obtained, the stronger becomes the desire to travel at a still greater speed. Railways have to go on rails, automobiles require well-made roads and even steamships have to sail in a certain course. To obviate all this, they are now engaged in perfecting aeroplanes. In the year 1909, when Bleriot, a French aeronaut, succeeded for the first time in crossing the English Channel in his monoplane from Calais to Dover—a distance of 20 miles in about 37 minutes—the enthusiasm of both the French and the English knew no bounds. He became the hero of the hour and his praises were sung by everybody. The public receptions given in his honour in Paris and London were hardly surpassed by triumphs held in honour of the conquering heroes and eminent statesmen. However, before many days were over, the other aeronauts overtook him, succeeded in performing still greater feats of sailing in the air, and cast his glory into the shade. Bleriot's name is now almost forgotten.

Inventions following inventions led the aeronauts to look out for still greater feats until some of them thought that the day was not far distant when they could overtake birds flying in the air at the rate of 180 miles an hour, and could perform the voyage between London and New York, a distance of about 3,000 miles, in 24 hours. Mr. Gandhi says that they forget that more haste means more waste.

All these facilities of travelling have made it possible for even men of ordinary means to travel in great comfort. In England, even the third class seats are cushioned. In the fast passenger trains, electric bells are provided. The passenger has simply to press the button from his seat when he requires any eatables or drinks, and a waiter appears and attends to his orders. The restaurant car attached to the train provides the most sumptuous meals at regular intervals. All that the traveller needs is a pocketful of gold. Sea voyages are not less comfortable. Some of the steamers are quite like floating palaces. They carry almost every article that is likely to be commanded by their patrons. To make life on board a complete holiday, the only thing that was missed by the passengers hitherto was a daily paper at the breakfast table. Even this requirement is being met in some of the trans-Atlantic steamers now-a-days, and when the Marconigraph installations are fitted in the other mail-liners, the day's news of the world will be printed and distributed daily on board for the benefit of the passengers.

All these inventions and discoveries, however, have not made man any more contented and happy than he was before. On the contrary, the more he gets, the more he wants, and the more exacting he becomes. He is becoming altogether restless, and is most unhappy when he has to sit still doing nothing. He wishes to be constantly on the move for new pleasures and new life. The concern of the rich is to get richer, and spend the money in objects that fascinate them. The poor, on the contrary, are being worked harder in order to provide the rich with the articles that contribute to their comforts and luxuries. The drivers of motor-buses are obliged to drive them at more than double the speed at which they used to drive the horse-buses formerly, in the busy thoroughfares of large cities, with the result that their lives are more or less lives of extreme nervous tension and they often suffer from nervous breakdown, necessitating absence from work for several months every year. Not long ago there was an article in one of the London papers, depicting the miserable condition of the motor-bus drivers. It stated that when they were employed in driving horse-buses, their lot was a pitiable one indeed, and yet they plied their business quite cheerfully. But since the motor-buses have got in, the men have to be all attention, they look quite pale and haggard, and have hardly any love for the work they do, or the life they lead.

Railways and steamers have also done a lot of mischief in India. The business of the cart-drivers and boat-pliers has almost slipped from their hands. Mr. Gandhi says that with the increased facilities of travelling, love for one's family, love for one's relations, love for one's community, love for one's country, and love for one's religion have considerably diminished, and instead, love of self and material comforts has correspondingly increased. Every one now-a-days desires to be instantaneously rich, and when his object cannot be served nearer home, he travels even to the very farthest corners of the earth. To make money anyhow is the object of the many. Max O'Rell, the author of 'John Bull and his Island,' says therein, that at the time of parting with his son, who was going to a distant part of the world to earn a living, the Scotch father gave him the following advice:—"Make money, honestly if you can, but make money." It is not to be wondered at, that one who leaves his own home and hearth behind to seek new pastures, can hardly think of being punctilious about the means that may have to be employed in order to achieve that end. Religion and morality no longer act on him as such strong deterrents from wrong-doing as when he was living in his own family or social group. Mr. Gandhi says from personal knowledge acquired while travelling in India that the ancient places of pilgrimage and worship have become places of wickedness since the advent of the railways, and that the people, having hardly any faith left in them, have not the same incentive to pilgrimage as they had in days gone by. The principal aim in going to a place of pilgrimage used to be to set apart so many days solely for religious worship and contemplation, and to undergo the trials and sufferings, while travelling often on foot, from one holy place to another. But in these days of quick travelling and greater facilities for obtaining the necessary provisions and all other daily requirements, many of the pilgrims simply rush from place to place, and return home within a week or a fortnight, in the false belief that they have performed their religious rites and duties. Surely, such pilgrimages cannot conduce to the purification of their souls.

The multiplication of railways has almost revolutionised the Indian character and Indian thought. Their intellectual, moral and religious ideas have received great shocks, and their economical condition has considerably deteriorated. Before the advent of the railways, the bulk of the population living in the villages were able to carry on their agricultural and other pursuits quite light-heartedly and cheerfully, and were able to produce enough for all their purposes without much difficulty. But in these days, a little drought, and they are at their wit's end. In old times, the harvests they reaped in good years were more than enough for the year's requirements, and the surplus used to be stored in the village granaries. But in these days of quick transit, most of the produce is sold as soon as it is ready, and when their small local stock is finished, they begin to import their food-stuffs from other places by railways. The double freight and other costs increase the price of the commodity, and thus living has become much more costly than before. In the countries of Europe, the additional facilities of transport have cheapened a great many articles of daily requirements, but in India the prices of all the necessaries of life have increased tremendously during the last twenty-five years, and in some cases they have more than doubled. The Government has appointed a Commission of inquiry on this subject.

Let us hope it will suggest some ameliorative remedies for the benefit of the poor ryots.

Mr. Gandhi believes that the commercial applications of modern sciences such as Physics, Mechanics, Chemistry, Electricity, Geology, Political Economy, Medicine, etc., have a very baneful effect on society, and that the institutions of Courts, Pleaders, etc., brings down humanity to a much lower level. Most of the modern institutions conduce to abnormal desires for riches and they tend to make man more materialistic than ever. With the growth of wealth on one side comes abnormal growth of poverty on the other. That is how the number of the unemployed is on the increase in the richest of the countries of Europe such as England and France. The peace of mind that pervaded all classes of society before the introduction of the modern sciences into daily use, is fast disappearing everywhere, and thus a number of diseases unknown in former times has found their way into the human system. These are the diseases due to modern conditions. They are also on the increase. Edward Carpenter in his book on "Civilization : Its Cause and Cure" says :—

"Anyone who would get an idea of the glorious being that is as a matter of fact being turned out by the present process should read Mr. Kay Robinson's article in the *Nineteenth Century* for May 1883, in which he prophesies (quite solemnly and in the name of science) that the human being of the future will be a toothless, bald, toeless creature with flaccid muscles and limbs almost incapable of locomotion."

Faced with the above conditions, some of the great thinkers of Europe are now-a-days devoting their time and energy to the spread of healthy literature on the evils of Industrialism and Commercialism and on the incalculable disadvantage which railways, steamships and other quick means of transit have brought about. The modern factory system, which draws thousands of people from their villages to exchange their open-air life for one in the close atmosphere of the workshops, is pictured by them as having no redeeming feature from the workman's point of view. Their theme is that the people should go back to land to develop agriculture and handicrafts, and to take to the simple life of their forefathers. Ruskin in England, Zola in France, and Tolstoy in Russia, besides a number of other writers, have written a number of treatises exposing the evils of modern civilization and the consequent degradation to humanity which it brings in its train. The Indian worshippers of modern civilization would do well to study some of the works of these great thinkers. To a careful student of the modern conditions, it is plain that the various inventions and discoveries over which there is so much boast, can do no good to the people, at any rate almost to 90 per cent. of them. The latter have to earn their daily livelihood in all countries and in all climates, from manual labour. If they are made the slaves of machinery, it is so much worse for them. There are people in India, who advocate the use of machinery in agriculture and in the manufacture of articles of daily use. If the old methods of agriculture, that have been in vogue in this country for thousands of years, were replaced by machinery, and if the ploughing, sowing, harvesting, etc., were done as in Canada or Australia, those engaged in the actual operations would become merely the slaves of the machinery, and a great many of the agriculturists would have to go to swell the number of the unemployed. Agriculture is directly and indirectly the sole means of subsistence for 80 per cent. of the Indian population. If machinery is introduced, it will take the place of from 90 to 95 per cent. of them. Woe to the people, if ever agricultural machinery comes to be introduced in India on any perceptible scale. The new conditions would undoubtedly drive the majority of the people into the streets, and the whole of the Indian social structure would crumble down to pieces.

The same thing applies to machinery in every other line of production. Not long ago, India was one of the largest manufacturing countries in the world. Its hand-loom fabrics were everywhere in demand. Macaulay says that "from the looms of Benares went forth the most delicate silks that adorned the halls of St. James and the Petit Trianon." That country now depends very largely on the stuffs sent out from Manchester, Glasgow, Hamburg and other manufacturing towns. But its hand-weaving industry has not fortunately been lost to the people. It was generally believed, and is generally believed by great many people even now, that hand-made stuffs could not stand in competition with machine-made things. This, however, is not borne out by experience. Thousands of weavers in Bengal, having been thrown out of work on account of foreign competition, were wandering about in search of employment, before the Swadeshi idea took hold of the people in that province. About five years ago almost all of them returned to their ancestral homes to follow their ancestral calling, and are to-day making heaps of stuffs, which are sold as soon as they are ready. The great advantage of hand-weaving industry is that it is carried on in the artisans' cottages, and that in spare moments the other members of the family can contribute their quota to swell their family earnings. This is the custom in every centre where hand-weaving is still going on. The import of foreign stuffs has thereby somewhat diminished. The object-lesson from this practical instance is that the industry is dying out, not so much on account of foreign competition, as for want of genuine home patronage on a large scale. The coarse but durable and elegant looking, as well as beautifully coloured home-made stuffs have to a very considerable extent been displaced by cheaper, finer and but fragile foreign stuffs. The real well-wishers of the country ought to use home-made stuffs even though apparently dearer, and give their patronage to this most deserving class of artisans. Wherever possible, they ought to foster this industry, as well as all other handicrafts, for the carrying on of which the people have not yet lost the necessary skill, but which they may lose, in course of time, if they do not receive sufficient patronage. The patronage needed should be given while there is yet time. The majority of those who take to English education in the hope of entering some kind of service, would certainly get on better, if they were to devote their attention to handicrafts, and acquire that delicacy of touch and sense (of the perception) of colour which is a peculiarity of the Indian artists. If these young men learn to use their limbs and artisans' tools more than they do their pens, the gain to the country would be immense. The years that are often frittered away in learning a foreign language at the expense of health and wealth would, in a great number of them, be better employed in the artisans' workshops. Many of those who die prematurely from nervous breakdowns due to hard study, would thus be saved to the country. Before modern mechanical appliances were invented, this country was known for its unrivalled skill in almost every kind of handicraft, and there is yet time to cultivate that skill and acquire that facility in handling the tools, that their forefathers did, and that some of the people do even now. If mechanical appliances were introduced into India in the same way as they are in Europe, it would not be long before the millions of her people would be ruined. The great advantage of the handicrafts is that the people can work them in their own cottages and that every member of the family can help them in their hours of leisure. Where a hundred men are required to do a certain amount of work by hand, probably 5 men will suffice to turn out the same amount of work by machinery. The result will be that in course of time, a very large percentage of them would be thrown out of employment. It is, therefore, the sacred duty of every Indian to encourage handicrafts as much as possible, and to leave the world's manufacturing work to those who care for it. The leading men in our Congresses and Conferences are mostly taken in by the glare of machinery, and, in and out of season, they recommend to their countrymen the use of machinery for the development of Indian arts and industries on a large scale. A number of them are interested in the working of them. Surely, they cannot contend that they are doing any good to the people, that is, the working classes from whom they exact as much work as they possibly can, for a mere pittance in the closed, stuffy and sometimes unbearable atmosphere of the workshops in the towns,—men who have necessarily to be separated from their family and friends to lead a monotonous and unhealthy existence there. A great many things are done in the name of the people, in which the latter's interests are far from beneficial. To those who are particularly interested in this subject, I would recommend Dr. A. K. Coomaraswamy's essays on National Idealism.

Mr Gandhi says that factories of the kind started in Europe are altogether unsuited to the Indian environment. According to his view, the greatest good of the greatest number could be secured by the development of cottage industries, such as at one time flourished in every nook and corner of India. The more this idea is brought home to the minds of the people, and the more it is brought into actual practice, the healthier will be our future growth. The more the people work in their own homes, and with their own families, the better is it for their moral and spiritual advancement. In the small Colonies at Phœnix and the newly-started Tolstoy Farm, Mr. Gandhi and his associates are working on this principle. Phœnix has been in existence for the last six or seven years. The Tolstoy Farm came into existence only last year. In the older Colony, the settlers have almost taken a vow of poverty. They live in very simple cottages, and pass a good deal of their time in the open air, doing gardening and agricultural work. They propose to devote some time to handicrafts also. Here they live upon the bare necessaries of life, put on just enough clothing that would protect them from cold and the effects of the climate, and inculcate these principles by personal example in the people they come in contact with. They have started a small school where they give their spare time to teaching their pupils the beauties of simple life. The *Indian Opinion* of Natal is a work of their joint labours. Their manhood is of a very high order. At the Tolstoy Farm, the principle is the same. For the present, only the passive resisters and their families are residing there. Most of them, including Mr. Gandhi, put in enough manual labour to earn their daily bread. The one great peculiarity of these institutions is that they foster the development of character. Indians could not do better than follow these men in their footsteps. They are real Swadeshists in every way, that is, in thought and action, in dress and diet, in religion and morals. Mr. Gandhi says that India could be regenerated only through the medium of Swadeshi ideas.

IDEALS IN EDUCATION.

Mr. Gandhi holds very definite and mature views in the matter of the education of the Indian youths, and it will not be out of place to mention them here in brief. He is of opinion that the system of education introduced in India on the basis of the recommendations of Lord Macaulay is most unsuited to the country. Most part of the time of an Indian boy or girl in the secondary school is spent in learning to translate his vernacular into English and *vice versa*, and yet after years of hard study, it cannot be said that many of them have more than a mere smattering of the knowledge of English. Most of those who subsequently go through the University studies show not much better results. After years of study, their knowledge of the foreign language is lamentably poor. A great many of them forget the subjects learnt through its medium soon after they have gone through their examinations. The system encourages cram in its very worst form. It does not lead to the development of the real man in them. Most of them acquire only a superficial knowledge of the foreign language, and do not trouble themselves much about their own mother tongue. If the subjects prescribed in the curricula of the various faculties were taught through the medium of their own mother tongue, they would certainly have a far better grasp of the subjects taught to them, and they would become better citizens. In the administration of the country, in its Law Courts and even in trade and commerce English should be replaced by Hindi or Hindusthani, which should be the *Lingua Franca* of India. This is one of the problems, on the solution of which the progress or otherwise of the country depends a great deal. In these days our English-educated men generally talk amongst themselves in English, and that in most cases is quite broken. They correspond with each other in English, almost of the same type. The proceedings of our congresses and conferences are all in English. Our best newspapers and magazines are published in English. In most cases we spend our leisure hours in the reading exclusively of the English literature. We prefer to dress as the Europeans do. We like to adopt their manners and customs in several ways. We very often think and even dream in English. We study the political constitution of England, and would like to introduce it whole-sale in the country if we could. In this way we strive to imitate them in every way. The majority are only able to see and judge of things very superficially, and at best can pick up their bad points.

The people in general take things as they find them. They look upon the man who has acquired some knowledge of English as "an educated man." One who can write and address public meetings in English is considered a very highly educated man. Knowledge of one's own language counts for nothing. Those well versed in it and other-wise respected, have often to eke out a precari-ous living, sometimes even by begging. The lot of the Thinkers, Poets, Authors, etc., is not very much better. The number of English-knowing Indians who care to read their own literature in their own tongue, is very small indeed. Men learned in the ancient literature of the country are very lightly esteemed. Sanskrit scholars and learned men who are able to expound the beauties of the old religious and philosophical works, are treated in this material world as superstitious men. The Shastries employed in the High Schools on a very scanty pay to teach Sanskrit, have to serve under men who have passed one or two University examinations, but who are hardly fit to be their pupils. Very often the very experts in this line are placed under the orders of young men who are just out of their teens. Mr. Gandhi deplores all that is going on in the name of higher education. His prescription is that every Indian ought to have a good knowledge of Sanskrit or Arabic, Hindi or Urdu besides that of his mother-tongue. The various subjects that the students wish to learn should be taught in their own vernaculars. Instead of increasing the number of English schools, and trying to spread English broadcast, the number of vernacular schools should be multiplied, and the knowledge of the vernaculars encouraged in every possible manner. He thinks it would be very much better if the whole of the educational machinery were subordinated to Indian requirements, and placed under Indian control, pure and simple. To diminish the craving for service, so baneful to their growth, it would be very necessary to divert their attention to the development of arts and industries also on the old lines. He says that the best way to elevate their manhood is to encourage them to earn their livelihood by the sweat of their brow. He has great faith in agriculture and believes that that life conduces to better health and more manly vigour. He has been directing his sons and nephews to this channel. He himself has given up practising as a lawyer, and is at present working like a common labourer on the Tolstoy Farm near Johannesburg. His life there is a model of simplicity and purity. Having passed through various phases of life and studied a great deal of human nature, his opinions are worth careful consideration. In the matter of education as it is imparted to-day in the schools and colleges, his convictions are very strong. Talking on the deplorable results of that education in most cases, he expressed himself as follows:—

"It is worth noting that by receiving English education, we have enslaved the nation. Hypocricy, tyranny, etc., have increased; English-knowing Indians have not hesitated to cheat and strike terror into the people. Now if we are doing anything for the people at all, we are paying only a portion of the debt due to them. If this state of things continues for a long time, posterity will, it is my firm opinion, condemn and curse us."

SOLVING THE HINDU-MAHOMEDAN PROBLEM.

No Indian in modern times has succeeded so well in bringing the Hindus and Mahomedans together on a common platform as Mr. Gandhi. That, in my opinion, is one of the greatest services that he has rendered to his country. In South Africa the two communities have been working in co-operation for several years past, and are thereby drawn closer to each other. In all important questions in which their interests as Indians are involved, they work almost with one mind. They have thus acquired a status in the country which, however much some of the white Colonists may like to ignore, is there and has to be counted as an important factor in South African politics. In India also there is practical unanimity with regard to their problems. The reason why the Resolution of the Honourable Mr. Gokhale on the stoppage of the Indian Indentured labour to Natal was supported by every Member of the Legislative Council last year, and why after one year's grace to the Union Government to mend matters, the Government of India declared their determination to put that Resolution in force from July next, was the result of the unanimity with which that question was always treated by the Hindus and Mahomedans residing in South Africa. The above declaration of the Government of India proves that the demands of the Indians were just, and that the attitude of the Union Government towards them was indefensible. This is no small victory from the Indian point of view, and that is due to the purity of motives with which Mr. Gandhi and his associates are working for the common welfare in that country.

Why could not we take a leaf from the noble example set to us by our brethren in South Africa in matters purely Indian? The Hindus and Mahomedans are the sons of the same soil and are nurtured almost upon the same culture. Their manners and customs and the very constitution of their society are almost identical. The laws of the British Government are applicable equally to both of them. Some of the institutions based upon modern civilization and particularly the educational machinery brought into requistion on that basis are injurious to Hindus and Mahomedans alike. The trade and commerce which otherwise might have been in the hands of the Indians is at present in foreign hands. The Civil and Military posts under the Government which might have been theirs, are in the hands of the Europeans. Both the communities have suffered equally from the extinction of purely Indian arts and Indian industries. The Pundits and Shastries learned in the ancient literature of the Hindus are in as bad plight as the Moulvis and Kazis versed in the literature dealing with the Mahomedan religion and Mahomedan law. In the law courts, where they have to resort to, in order to seek justice, the language difficulty is the same to both, and the litigation there is equally costly to them. The members of both the communities have to pay the same taxes to the Government. The Hindu gains and losses under the altered conditions in which the country is placed are no more and no less than those of the Mahomedan. The improvement of agriculture, the promotion of Indian arts and industries, the introduction of a better and more suitable system of education, and the moral and religious advance of both the communities in their peculiar ways, would be as advantageous to the Hindus as to the Mahomedans. For the good of the country does it matter at all if their religious faiths are not the same? How does it affect the interests of the country at large, if one part of its people worships in a temple, and the other part prays in a mosque? Surely, that is a matter which must be left solely to the private judgment of the individuals. In the same way, if a few more posts under the Government are given to Mahomedans and a few less to the Hindus, that cannot in any way clash with the interests of the country. All over the continent of America, the English, the French, the Germans, the Russians, the Austrians, the Italians, the Spaniards, the Portuguese, and the people of other European countries live side by side. They belong to the thousand and one creeds into which Christianity is divided. Some of them acknowledge the Jewish faith to which at one time the former was deadly opposed. None the less they all feel, and rightly too, that they are American citizens, and not English or French or others, as the case may be. They do not bring in their private differences and dissensions in affairs of general importance. Why should not we follow their good example? The Indian Mahomedans have no other country but India which they can call their Mother country. Why should they not feel for it just as much as the Hindus, and why should the two not work in co-operation with each other? When the British Government decided to allow the Mahomedans a few more seats in the Legislative Councils, the Hindus were greatly perturbed, and they started holding meetings in different parts of the country to protest against the arrangement. It is very difficult to realize how by that action of the Government, the Hindu community as such could suffer any loss, and the Mahomedan community as such could gain any advantage. Why should the Hindus be at all displeased at the action of the Government? And after all, who among the Hindus are displeased? There is no doubt that the agitation against the said arrangement was to a very large extent fostered by men who are personally interested in the elections to the seats on the Legislative Councils. How a Hindu Member in any of these Councils can work more for the good of the Hindus and a Mahomedan Member for the good of the Mahomedans, is a question to which those who protest ought to give more than a passing thought. The dissensions caused by such sentiments in the two communities are eating into the very vitals of the nation. Properly considered, there is no such thing as the gain of one community at the expense of the other. The differences that may arise between them should be decided by mutual forbearance and the policy of give-and-take. The moment they bring themselves to a more rational frame of mind and cease to desire precedence over each other, but desire instead precedence as a nation, over other nations, and think independently of their respective castes, creed, and colour, the interests of the country would begin to advance by leaps and bounds, and the religious, moral, social and political progress of the different Indian communities would be as substantial as her best sons would crave for. Mr. Gandhi has expressed his views on this problem very often. Their gist is contained in a letter written by him to a leading Mahomedan gentleman in reply to his. It is as follows:—"I never realise any distinction between a Hindu and a Mahomedan. To my mind both are the sons of Mother India. I know that the Hindus are in a numerical majority, and that they are believed to be more advanced in knowledge and education. Accordingly, they should be glad to give way so much the more to their Mahomedan brethren. As a man of truth, I honestly believe that Hindus should yield up to the Mahomedans what the latter desire, and that they should rejcice in so doing. We can expect unity only if such mutual large-heartedness is displayed. When the Hindus and Mahomedans act towards each other as brothers sprung of the same mother, then alone can there be unity, then only can we hope for the dawn of India."

THE INDIAN INDENTURED LABOUR.

Of late, the question of Indian Indentured labour has attracted a great deal of attention in this country as well as outside it. This is due to Mr Gandhi. He has had unique opportunities for studying the question. He is of opinion that the root-cause of most of the sufferings that the Indians have had to undergo in South Africa, is the Indenture Law passed by the Government of India. The Colonies that have been allowed to exploit Indian labour since the law came into force, have been trying to treat the free Indians also that have gone to settle down there as if they belonged to the same class of society as the indentured labourers. The general appellation given to all Indians in these colonies is "coolies", no matter what rank of society they come from. It is enough that they come from the same country, and perhaps belong to the same stock. The great majority of the European Colonists treat the Indian population living side by side with them with contumely and feelings of disgust. Wherever they are, they are treated as men belonging to inferior races. On my return from Europe in 1898, I took the old route to India, and passed through the Cape Colony, the Orange River Colony (then Orange Free State), the Transvaal and Natal before embarking again at Durban for Colombo. I was not in Cape Town for more than two hours, before they made me feel that I was in a place where the colour of the skin counted for everything and man nothing. I was at once convinced that the journey could not be a pleasant one to him who did not wear white skin. The men in charge of the Hotels to which I went to secure a room for a few days' stay, invariably told me there was no room there. At first, I believed their statement to be true, but when I had gone over a dozen of them, it dawned on me that they were not willing to take a coloured man into their premises. My experiences in Kimberly and other places were almost the same. Had not the Government of India passed the Indenture Law and had the Natal European Colonists never been allowed to grow fat on cheap Indian labour, to-day there would have been no Indian problem at all in South Africa. The few Indians that would have gone there for pleasure or business, would have found its doors as wide open to them as they are at present in every country of Europe.

The thinking part of the people of Europe look upon Indian civilization with feelings of respect, and India as the mother of all civilizations. They treat Indians as their equals. Nowhere is any difficulty experienced by them while travelling or residing there. Some of the French and German savants spend their lives in the study of the ancient literature and philosophy of India and consider it a high honour to learn at the feet of the great masters India has produced. If Europe ever required Indian Indentured labour, and if the Government of India allowed it to exploit that labour, it would not be long before those Indians who were settled down in the various parts thereof began to be looked upon as "coolies".

By virtue of the Act, the wily and often beggarly Indian recruiters of the White Colonists of Natal are able to induce the poor and ignorant but home-loving labouring classes of the Indian villages in certain districts, to agree to temporary slavery in a far-off land. The labourers are given all sorts of false hopes and promises, and are made to believe that they have simply to go there in order to obtain nuggets of gold, which they can do by simply digging the land which is represented to them as full of riches of all sorts. As soon as they yield to these and similar temptations they are made to affix their signatures to a document binding them for five years to serve unknown masters in distant lands, of which they have no conception whatever, for a mere pittance. Legally they are supposed to have voluntarily entered into the contract, and to be able to understand its terms fully, though the document is so worded, as all legal documents are, that even lawyers would not find it easy to interpret it always properly. When they reach Natal, the Protector of Immigrants assigns them to different masters. Some of them are sent to work on tea, coffee and sugar estates, some in coal mines, some for the municipalities, and some are sent to work for the Government on railways and other services. The masters are not all alike. Some of them have obtained wide notoriety for selfishness and greed, and punish the men severely for the most trivial faults. The labourers are bound to serve any of the employers to whom they are assigned. The men being ignorant of the country, its language, etc., and otherwise very simple, have to undergo innumerable hardships during the period of indenture. On some of the plantations, they are looked upon as mere beasts of burden and are treated worse than cattle. Mr. H. S. L. Polak in his book "The Indians of South Africa," while writing on this subject, says:—

"Between the master and the servant, under such a law, there can be no human relationship, save such as may often be observed between the owner and his cattle. And as a matter of fact, the Indian labourer is often regarded by his employer as of less account than a good beast, for the latter costs money to replace, whereas the former is a cheap commodity. The system too is unfair in its incidence, for the balance of advantage in the contract of service lies always with the employer and never with the employed. So long as the breach of contract on the part of the labourer is always (and on that of the employer seldom) regarded as a criminal and not as a civil matter, it is impossible to regard Indenture in any light other than that of a system perilously approaching one of servile conditions, and this quite independently of what may obtain in other parts of the world, where conditions may be better or worse."

If the master to whom a particular labourer is assigned is inhuman and treats him unfairly or cruelly, the latter must, in the first place, obtain the permission of a neighbouring Magistrate to proceed against the former. This is not always easy. What his troubles and difficulties in the matter are may be better told in the words of Mr. Polak. In his book quoted above he graphically describes the predicament in which the labourer that is wronged by his master is placed when he is obliged to seek justice in the Courts of Law, and the difficulties he has in obtaining it in that Colony. He says:—"Take the case where an employer ill-treats a labourer. The man is on his way to make a complaint when he is arrested by a Kaffir policeman, who takes him back to his employer, with what results may be better imagined than described. Should he succeed in reaching the local Magistrate unmolested, he is required to satisfy that functionary of his having a *primâ facie* case against his employer. If the Magistrate happens to be a friend of the employer, a powerful man in the district, he may refuse to issue the Pass authorising the man to complain to the Protector, and may return him under escort to the employer, the complainant having to bear the cost of such return. Should the latter from fear or ignorance fail to go to the Magistrate, but proceed direct to the Protector, that official's first demand is for the Pass to make complaint, and as this is not forthcoming, the unfortunate man is placed before the Durban Magistrate and convicted for the breach of the above rules. Suppose, however, that he has done all that by law he is required to do, and has safely arrived at the Protector's office. The Protector having taken the man's written deposition, and before investigation, will order the man's return to his employer. Knowing what to expect there, and realising that his complaint is almost certain in these circumstances to be ascribed to causes other than the real ones, he positively refuses to return. He is then sent before the Magistrate by the Protector, and is convicted and sentenced as previously described. Even then he may be returned to his employer at his own expense, and may find his complaint unredressed and his last condition worse than his first. Has all this nothing to do with the heavy suicide rate? Men have been known to attempt suicide in the Magistrate's Court rather than be made to return to their employers, and there has been only the most perfunctory inquiry."

The Magistrates mostly decide their complaints to be false or frivolous. The accused is hardly ever punished for ill-treatment and cruelty. The complainant from the very nature of the circumstances in which he is placed, is unable to offer sufficient corroborative evidence to prove his statement. His fellow-workers, who are witnesses of the tragedy, are unwilling to appear and give evidence against their master, however wrong he may have been, for fear of a worse fate to themselves. The man's life becomes only more miserable for having ventured to seek justice in that manner.

In other respects also, the life of one who has once been an indentured labourer is often pitiable. Having spent from five to ten of the best years of his life under indenture in a foreign country, when repatriated as a large number of them are, he finds life much harder in his village than before. He has practically to start it again. And those out of them who prefer to stay on in the Colony for one reason or another, are obliged to pay, according to Mr. Polak, "a minimum taxation of £7 per annum to the State upon an average monthly income of twenty shillings, rent in addition to this."

The aforesaid conditions of life are such as would demoralise anybody. Situated as he is, an indentured Indian would be more than human if he does not go down morally and religiously from day to day.

The above are some of the grounds on which Mr. Gandhi advocated the total abolition of the Indenture Law in force in India. The conditions of service are not far removed from those of slavery as it was known before the slave trade was abolished. In some respects, the condition of the slaves of old was decidedly better than that of the Indentured Indian labourer of to-day. In 1908, at a mass meeting of the Natal Indians, a resolution was passed urging the

Government of India to stop indentured labour to Natal. Mr. Polak, whose name will always remain associated with that of Mr. Gandhi in this matter, at the various meetings that were held in India in 1909-10 to discuss the South African problem, brought home to the minds of the people and the Government, the troubles and hardships from which the indentured labourers suffered. Thus came about the acceptance of the Hon'ble Mr. Gokhale's resolution in 1910 in favour of the stoppage of the indentured labour to Natal and the promise of stopping it altogether by the Government of India from July 1st of the present year.

In passing, I may just remark that Natal is not the only Colony where the conditions of indenture press hard upon the Indians. The grievances are almost similar in every Colony that is allowed to exploit Indian labour. Indians ought not to rest satisfied until the Indenture Law passed by the Government of India is altogether abrogated from the Statute Book.

Any account of Mr. Gandhi would be quite incomplete that does not mention his views on religion. His personal life is nothing if it is not based on the very highest principles of religion and morality. Mr. Doke has given a very vivid description of his religious beliefs and practices in his book, and I would earnestly request its readers to go through that particular chapter with more than their usual attention. Mr. Gandhi acts on the grand principle that all of us, whether we are called Hindus, Mahomedans, Buddhists or Christians, or whether we hail from the Punjab, the United Provinces, Bengal, Bombay or Madras, nay, from any other part of this planet, are sons of one and the same Maker. He has the same love and sympathy for them all, as he has for his own kith and kin. Mr. Doke has mentioned various incidents in his life in which his practice has been found to be always in consonance with his preaching. The one virtue which distinguishes Mr. Gandhi from all others is that he never puts forward an idea or extols an action, which he himself would not be prepared to act upon when circumstances required him to do so. In fact, he practises himself first what he desires to preach to others. Very few have his courage of conviction and once he believes the truth of any particular line of conduct, no risk, nothing, will deter him from going on, on that path without in the least caring whether anyone else believes in it at all, or is prepared to follow him in his footsteps.

Speaking to a mixed gathering of Hindus and Mahomedans at the mosque in Johannesburg, he expressed the following idea about what he meant by religion.

"By religion I do not mean formal religion or customary religion, but that religion that underlies all religions, which brings us face to face with our Maker."

RELIGION AND LOVE.

From the special study that he has made of the various religious faiths, he is convinced that the elementary principles of all religions are one and the same. He says that the way to serve the

Maker and to attain eternal salvation, is one and the same for all, whether they profess Hinduism, Mahomedanism, Christianity, Buddhism, Judaism, Zoroastrianism, Confucianism, or any other faith. The great object of religion ought to be, and as a matter of fact is, to produce harmony between man and man.

Mr. Gandhi's great principle of life has been, "to conquer hatred by love." It is no exaggeration to say that he is probably the only one among living men who is able to practise this doctrine to the very letter. He has almost regulated his daily life on this principle. Mr. Doke has given a number of instances in his book where he shows how, through all sorts of difficulties and adversities, he has always stuck to it. The successes, and one may say failures also, that Mr. Gandhi has had during his eventful career, are due to his following it in every path of life. Having no feelings of hatred or spite towards anyone, men who are politically opposed to his views show deference to him in private, and are often attracted towards him by his personality. Even General Smuts, who is so bitter against all Asiatics, is reported to have a great regard for his personality and has, in one or two instances, given practical proofs of it. The coterie of men who are working with him from day to day in Johannesburg, belong to different nationalities and different religious faiths. But for the help he was able to secure from Europeans like Messrs. Doke, Hosken Ritch, Polak, Kallenbach, etc., and Asiatics like Messrs. Quinn, Cachalia, Dawood Mahomed, Rustonji, Thambi Naidu, etc., hailing from different parts of Europe and Asia, he would not have been able to achieve half of what he has done. It is his daily practice of the above doctrine that brings him the co-operation of those who feel for the down-trodden and the oppressed. He has declared his views very often on this question. The following extract from the message that he sent to the Indian National Congress at Lahore held in 1909, clearly shows his idea on the subject:—

"The sons of Hindustan, who are in the Transvaal, are showing that they are capable of fighting for an ideal pure and simple. The methods adopted in order to secure relief are also equally pure and equally simple. Violence in any shape or form is entirely eschewed. They believe that self-suffering is the only true and effective means to procure lasting reforms. They endeavour to meet and conquer hatred by love. They oppose the brute or physical force by soul force. They hold that loyalty to an earthly sovereign or an earthly constitution is subordinate to loyalty to God and his constitution. In interpreting God's constitution through their conscience, they admit that they may possibly be wrong. Hence, in resisting or disregarding these man-made laws, which they consider to be inconsistent with the eternal laws of God, they accept with resignation the penalties provided by the former, and trust to the working of time and to the best in human nature to make good their position. If they are wrong they alone suffer and the established order of things continues."

MR. GANDHI'S CONFESSION OF FAITH.

The more Mr. Gandhi becomes known to

Europeans, the more is he appreciated by them. The fact that Lord Ampthill, a prominent nobleman of England, one of the late Governors of Madras and for some time Viceroy of India, has written a very sympathetic preface to Mr. Gandhi's life by Mr. Doke, speaks volumes. Those who come in personal contact with him are at once convinced of the purity of his mind and his high mission. The various lectures that he delivered in London during his last trip, were attended by a great many Englishmen and Anglo-Indians in the leading ranks, and were highly spoken of by them. Some of the Transvaal politicians and public men who were at one time very bitter against him, are now among his best friends. All that is due to his humanitarian views and actions; he believes that the longstanding racial prejudices and jealousies between the Europeans and Asiatics are very detrimental to both. He seems to consider that one of his missions is to promote harmony and sympathy between them, and he is always working upon that basis.

Mr. Doke's remarks about the goal which Mr. Gandhi has in view, are worth very careful perusal and study. Mr. Doke's concluding remarks in his book show how pure are Mr. Gandhi's ideals and how lofty are his aims. While Mr. Gandhi was being marched to the Johannesburg jail during his second incarceration from the Court House, where he had been summoned to give evidence in a case, he was found very much engrossed in his thoughts. Mr. Doke in trying to guess what they possibly could be, first asks whether they were about the horrible place he was being sent to, but on second thought he says :—

"No, not that; it is another Jerusalem which he faces steadfastly. It is such a city as all inspired men see, and to build whose walls they still 'endure the cross, despising shame.' A holy city, already come down from God out of Heaven, forming unrecognised, unseen by worldly souls, amid the squalour of to-day, wherever God's children are. A new Jerusalem whose beautiful gates are ever open to all nations; where no colour-bar is permitted to challenge the Indian and no racial prejudice to daunt the Chinese, into whose walls even an Asiatic may build those precious stones which one day will startle us with their glory."

That he is not thinking of building such a Jerusalem on paper only is quite evident from the manner in which he has applied himself to the task. He is busy at it the whole day barring the hours of sleep and food. Even the former he considers so much waste of time, and spends as little after it as would be absolutely necessary to maintain his body in a fairly healthy condition. How he means to do it may be gauged from the following extracts from a letter to his friend, as quoted in "M. K. Gandhi" published by Mr. Natesan. It is styled the confession of his faith, and runs as follows :—

(1) There is no impassable barrier between East and West.

(2) There is no such thing as Western or European civilization, but there is a modern civilization which is purely material.

(3) The people of Europe, before they were touched by modern civilization had much in common with the people of the East; anyhow the people of India, and even to-day Europeans who are not touched by modern civilization are far better able to mix with the Indians than the offspring of that civilization.

(4) It is not the British people who are ruling India, but it is modern civilization, through its railways, telegraphs, telephones and almost every invention, which has been claimed to be a triumph of civilization.

(5) Bombay, Calcutta, and other chief cities of India are the real plague spots.

(6) If British rule was replaced to-morrow by Indian rule based on modern methods, India would be no better except that she would be able then to retain some of the money that is drained away to England; but then India would only become a second or fifth edition of Europe or America.

(7) East and West can only and really meet when the West has thrown overboard modern civilization; but that meeting would be an armed truce, even as it is between, say, Germany and England, both of which nations are living in the Hall of Death in order to avoid being devoured the one by the other.

(8) It is simply impertinence for any man or any body of men to begin or contemplate reform of the whole world. To attempt to do so by means of highly artificial and speedy locomotion, is to attempt the impossible.

(9) Increase of material comforts, it may be

generally laid down, does not in any way whatsoever conduce to moral growth.

(10) Medical Science is the concentrated essence of Black Magic. Quackery is infinitely preferable to what passes for high medical skill.

(11). Hospitals are the instruments that the Devil has been using for his own purpose, in order to keep his hold on his kingdom. They perpetrate vice, misery, and degradation, and real slavery. I was entirely off the track when I considered that I should receive a medical training. It would be sinful for me in any way whatsoever to take part in the abominations that go on in the hospitals. If there were no hospitals for venereal diseases, or even for consumptives, we should have less consumption and less sexual vice amongst us.

(12) India's salvation consists in unlearning what she has learnt during the past fifty years. The Railways, Telegraphs, Hospitals, Lawyers, Doctors, and such like have all to go, and the so-called upper classes have to learn to live conscientiously and religiously, and deliberately, the simple pleasant life, knowing it to be a life-giving true happiness.

(13) India should wear no machine-made clothing whether it comes out of European mills or Indian mills.

(14) England can help India to do this, and then she will have justified her hold on India. There seem to be many in England to-day who think likewise.

(15) There was true wisdom in the sages of old having so regulated society as, to limit the material condition of the people; the rude plough

of perhaps five thousand years ago is the plough of the husbandman to-day. There lies salvation. People live long, under such conditions, in comparative peace much greater than Europe has enjoyed after having taken up modern activity, and I feel that every enlightened man, certainly every Englishman, if he chooses, may learn this truth and act according to it.

It is the true spirit of passive resistance that has brought me to the above almost definite conclusions. As a passive resister, I am unconcerned whether such a gigantic reformation, shall I call it, can be brought about among people who derive their satisfaction from the present mad rush. If I realize the truth of it, I should rejoice in following it, and, therefore, I could not wait until the whole body of people had commenced. All of us who think likewise have to take the necessary step, and the rest, if we are in the right, must follow. The theory is there; our practice will have to approach it as much as possible. Living in the midst of the rush, we may not be able to shake ourselves free from all taint. Every time I get into a railway car or use a motor-bus, I know that I am doing violence to my sense of what is right. I do not fear the logical result of that basis. The visiting of England is bad, and any communication between South Africa and India by means of ocean's grey-hounds is also bad, and so on. You and I can outgrow these things in our present bodies but the chief thing is to put our theory right. You will be seeing there all sorts and conditions of men. I, therefore, feel that I should no longer withhold from you what

I call the progressive step I have taken mentally. If you agree with me, then it will be your duty to tell the revolutionaries and everybody else that the freedom they want, or they think they want, is not to be obtained by killing people or doing violence, but by setting themselves right, and by becoming and remaining truly Indian. Then the British rulers will be servants and not masters. They will be trustees and not tyrants, and they will live in perfect peace with the whole of the inhabitants of India. The future, therefore, lies not with the British race, but with the Indians themselves, and if they have sufficient self-abnegation, and abstemiousness, they can make themselves free this very moment, and when we have arrived in India at the simplicity which is still ours largely and which was ours entirely until a few years ago, it will still be possible for the best Indians and the best Europeans to see one another throughout the length and breadth of India, and act as the leaven. When there was no rapid locomotion, teachers and preachers went on foot, from one end of the country to the other, braving all dangers not for pleasures, not for recruiting their health, (though all that followed from their tramps) but for the sake of humanity. Then were Benares and other places of pilgrimage, holy cities, whereas to-day they are an abomination.

You will recollect you used to rate me for talking to my children in Gujarati. I now feel more and more convinced that I was absolutely right in refusing to talk to them in English; fancy a Gujarati writing to another Gujarati in English, which as you would properly say, he mispronounces and writes ungrammatically. I should certainly never commit the ludicrous blunders in writing in Gujarati that I do in writing or speaking in English. I think that when I speak in English to an Indian or a foreigner, I in a measure unlearn the language. If I want to learn it well and if I want to attune my ear to it, I can only do so by talking to an Englishman, and by listening to an Englishman speaking."

I have known Mr. Gandhi for over twenty-two years very intimately. During all that time I have found that the one great difference between him and others is, that once he is convinced that a particular line of conduct, as tested by the highest canons of morality and the strictest doctrines of religion, is correct, it will not be long before he adopts it for himself as his daily practice, if he has not already been observing it. He says that if you wish the good of those you come in contact with, the only way to achieve the end is to be good yourself. Self-improvement and self-culture are his ideals. He always acts upon the proverb "Example is better than precept" and that is how all his theories and practice are blended so harmoniously one with another in his daily life. No earthly temptations are too strong for him, and none of them can make him swerve from the noble path that he has chalked out for himself. It is no exaggeration to say that in this age of materialism it is not possible to come across another man who lives the Ideal life he preaches.

The Hon. Mr. Gokhale's Speeches.

THIS is the first collection of his speeches and may claim to be fairly exhaustive, no important pronouncement of his having been omitted. The book contains four parts and an appendix. The first part includes all his utterances in the Supreme Legislative Council and in the Bombay Legislative Council; the second, all his Congress Speeches, including his Presidential Address at Benares; the third, speeches in appreciation of Hume, Naoroji, Ranade, Mehta and Bonnerjee; the fourth, miscellaneous speeches delivered in England and India. The Appendix contains the full text of his evidence both in chief and in cross-examination before the Welby Commission and various papers. These cover nearly a quarter of a century of a most strenuous, selfless and active public life and embrace the whole range of topics that have engaged and are still engaging the attention of the public. Full of instruction on every point and breathing in every line the moral fervour which is Mr. Gokhale's supreme characteristic, this volume, the publishers venture to hope, will command wide popularity.

Crown 8vo., 1,100 pp., Cloth Gilt. Price Rs. 3.

To Subscribers of the *Indian Review*, Rs. 2-8.

Dadabhai Naoroji's Speeches and Writings.

This is the most exhaustive and comprehensive collection of his speeches and writings. No speech or writing of importance has been omitted. It contains among others his three Congress presidential addresses and other speeches delivered in the Congress; all his speeches in the House of Commons; a selection from his speeches delivered in England and India during his many laborious campaigns; a collection of his papers, essays and statements to various Commissions, such as the Welby Commission, Indian Currency Committee, Fawcett Committee on Indian Finance, Famine Commission, etc. With a portrait.

Price Rs. Two.

To Subscribers of the "Indian Review," Rs. 1-8.

G. A. NATESAN & CO., ESPLANADE, MADRAS.

Aspects of the Vedanta

CONTENTS:

The Vedanta—Some Reasons for Study.
The Late Mr. N. Vythinatha Aiyar, M. A.

Veda and the Vedanta.
The Late Prof. Max Müller.

Vedanta Toward All Religions.
Swami Abhedananda.

The Vedanta in Outline.
Pandit Sitanath Tattvabhushan.

The Vedanta Religion.
Professor M. Rangachariar, M. A.

The Ethics of the Vedanta.
The Late Mr. N. Vythinatha Aiyar, M. A.
Rao Bahadur Vasudeva J. Kirtikar.

The Philosophy of the Vedanta.
Dr. Paul Deussen.

The Vedanta Philosophy.
Swami Vivekananda.

The Vedantic Doctrine of the Future Life.
Pandit Sitanath Tattvabhushan.

The Vedanta: Its Theory and Practice.
Swami Saradananda.

The Vedanta for the World.
Swami Vivekananda.

PRICE AS. 12.

To Subscribers of the *Indian Review*, As. 8.

—:o:—

☛ *The Annual Subscription to the "INDIAN REVIEW" is Rs. 5 (five). Subscription can commence from any month. Any one, who wishes to buy books at the reduced rates, must remit Rs. 5, one year's subscription to the "Review," in advance. Send a postage stamp for As. Two for a free specimen copy.*

G. A. NATESAN & CO., ESPLANADE, MADRAS.

Swami Vivekananda.

AN EXHAUSTIVE & COMPREHENSIVE COLLECTION OF

HIS SPEECHES AND WRITINGS.

This publication is the first of its kind. It is the first exhaustive and comprehensive collection of the works of Swami Vivekananda hitherto published. It contains, among others, his eloquent character-sketch of "My Master"; his celebrated lecture at the great Parliament of Religions at Chicago; all the important and valuable speeches delivered in England, America and India on Gnana Yoga, Bhakti Yoga, Karma Yoga, Vedanta, and Hinduism; Selection from the inspiring speeches he gave in reply to Addresses of Welcome that were presented to him at different towns and cities in India, during his historic journey from Colombo to Almora, on his return from America; a choice collection of the contributions of the Swami to various papers and periodicals hitherto not available in book form; some of his private letters to friends; and a selection from his poems.

DETAILED CONTENTS.—My Master; Hinduism as a Religion; Reply to the Addresses of Congratulations from Madras and Calcutta; The Ideal of Universal Religion; God in Everything; Immortality; Is the Soul Immortal; The Freedom of the Soul; Maya and Illusion; Maya and the Conception of God; Maya and Freedom; The Real and the Apparent Man; The Absolute and Manifestation; Unity in Diversity; The Cosmos; The Macrocosm; Realization; Karma-Yoga; Metaphysics in India; Re-incarnation; Bhakti or Devotion; Vedanta; The Vedanta in Indian Life; The Mission of the Vedanta; The Sages of India; Christ: The Messenger; The Relation of Buddhism to Hinduism; The True Method of Social Reform; The Reform of Caste; Education on National Lines; The Conquest of the World by Indian Thought; The Himalayas; Max Müller: A Vedantist; Japan Poems. Contains also *Four Portraits.* **PRICE RS. 2.**

To Subscribers of the "Review", Rs. 1-8.

G. A. NATESAN & CO., ESPLANADE, MADRAS.

M. K. GANDHI: A GREAT INDIAN.

This is a Sketch of the Life of Mr. M. K. Gandhi, one of the most eminent and self-sacrificing men that Modern India has produced. It describes the early days of Mr. M. K. Gandhi's life, his mission and work in South Africa, his character, his strivings, and his hopes. A perusal of this Sketch, together with the selected speeches and addresses that are appended, gives a peculiar insight into the springs of action that have impelled this remarkable and saintly man to surrender every material thing in life for the sake of an ideal that he ever essays to realise, and will be a source of inspiration to those who understand that statesmanship, moderation, and selflessness are the greatest qualities of a patriot. The Sketch contains an illuminating investigation into the true nature of passive resistance by Mr. Gandhi, which may be taken as an authoritative expression of the spirit of the South African struggle. (*With a portrait of Mr. Gandhi.*)

Price As. Four.

THE INDIANS OF SOUTH AFRICA.

Helots within the Empire! How they are Treated.

By H. S. L. Polak, Editor "*Indian Opinion.*"

This book is the first extended and authoritative description of the Indian Colonists of South Africa, the treatment accorded to them by their European fellow-colonists, and their many grievances. The First Part is devoted to a detailed examination of the disabilities of Indians in Natal, the Transvaal, the Orange River Colony, the Cape Colony, Southern Rhodesia, and the Portuguese Province of Mozambique. Part II. entitled "A Tragedy of Empire," describes the terrible struggle of the last three years in the Transvaal, and contains an appeal to the people of India. To these are added a number of valuable appendices.

Price Re. 1. To Subscribers of the "Review," As. 12.

G. A. NATESAN & CO., ESPLANADE, MADRAS.

INDIAN TALES.

AMUSING READING :—As. Four Each.

NEW INDIAN TALES.—Nineteen amusing and instructive tales. By Mr. C. Hayavadana Rau, Fellow of the Anthropological Institute, London. Price As. 4.

TALES OF RAYA AND APPAJI.—By T. M. Sundaram. 16 amusing and instructive stories. The stories are characterised by a great deal of wit and humour. Price As. 4.

TALES OF KOMATI WIT AND WISDOM.—Twenty-five amusing and instructive stories. By C. Hayavadana Rau, B. A., B. L. Price As. 4.

TALES OF TENNALI RAMAN.—The famous Court Jester of Southern India. 21 Amusing Stories. By Pandit S. M. Natesa Sastri. Third Edition. As. 4.

FOLKLORE OF THE TELUGUS.—A collection of forty-two highly amusing and instructive tales. By G. R. Subramiah Pantulu. Price As. 4.

TALES OF MARIADA RAMAN. (21 Amusing Stories.) By P. Ramachandra Row Avergal, Retired Statutory Civilian. Second Edition. Price As. 4.

THE SON-IN-LAW ABROAD, and other Indian folk-tales of Fun, Folly, Cleverness, Cunning, Wit, and Humour. By P. Ramachandra Rao, B. A., B. L., Retired Statutory Civilian. Second Edition. As. 4.

MAITREYI.

A VEDIC STORY IN SIX CHAPTERS.

BY PANDIT SITANATH TATTVABHUSHAN.

Indian Mirror.—The Author has recalled to life the dead bones of a very ancient and classical anecdote, and embellished it with his own imagination and philosophical disquisition. Pandit Sitanath has made the Maitreyi of the Vedic age as she should be—catholic, stout-hearted and intellectual and has through her mouth introduced and discussed many intricate, philosophical and social topics. We wish this little book every success.

SECOND EDITION. As. Four.

G. A. NATESAN & CO., ESPLANADE, MADRAS.

The Swadeshi Movement.

A SYMPOSIUM BY

Representative Indians and Anglo-Indians.

CONTENTS:—Dadabhai Naoroji; H. H. The Gaekwar of Baroda; The Hon. Mr. G. K. Gokhale; The Hon. Dr. Rash Behari Ghose; Hon. Sir Vitaldas Damodar Thackersey; The Hon. Md. Yusuf Khan Bahadur; Mrs. Annie Besant; Rajah Peary Mohun Mukerjee; Sister Nivedita; Mr. Lala Lajpat Rai; Dewan Bahadur K. Krishnaswamy Row; The Hon. Mr. Harikishen Lal; Babu Surendranath Banerjee; Rai Bahadur Lala Baij Nath; Dewan Bahadur Ragunatha Row; Romesh Chunder Dutt, C.I.E., I.C.S.; Mr. A. Chaudhuri; Hon. Mr. Parekh; Mr. D. E. Wacha; Hon. Pandit Madan Mohan Malaviya; Mr. Aswini Kumar Datta; The Hon. Mr. V. Krishnaswamy Iyer; Hon. Mr. Ambica Charan Muzumdar; Mr. Myron H. Phelps; Dewan Bahadur Ambalal S. Desai; Mr. G. S. Arundale; Sir Charles Elliot, K.C.M.G.; Mr. David Gostling; Rajah Prithwipal Singh; Rai Bahadur P. Ananda Charlu, C.I.E.; Sir E. C. Buck, K.C.S.I.; Dr. Ananda K. Coomaraswamy; Mr. Mujibur Rahman; Abdul Rasul, Esq., *Bar.-at-Law*; Babu Tara Prasanna Mukerji; Dewan Bahadur Govindaraghava Iyer; Mr. Abdul Halim Ghuznavi; Rao Bahadur R. N. Mudholkar; His Honor Sir Herbert T. White; Mr. Charles W. McKinn; Mr. Bal Gangadhar Tilak; Mr. Hemendra Prasad Ghose; Pandit Rambaj Dutt; Mr. Mushir Hosain Kidwai, *Bar.-at-Law.*

The book also contains the views of, H. E. Lord Minto, H. E. Sir Arthur Lawley, H. H. Sir Andrew Fraser and Lord Ampthill. Price Annas Twelve.

☞ *The Annual Subscription to the "INDIAN REVIEW" is Rs. 5 (five). Subscription can commence from any month Any one, who wishes to buy books at the reduced rates, must remit Rs. 5, one year's subscription to the "Review," in advance. Send a postage stamp for As. Two for a free specimen copy.*

G. A. NATESAN & CO., ESPLANADE, MADRAS.

Published by

Facsimile Publisher
Ashok Vihar, Delhi-110052 (India)
Website: www.facsimilepublishers.com

Distributed by

Gyan Books Pvt. Ltd.
5, Ansari Road, Daryaganj, New Delhi-110002 (India)
E-mail: books@gyanbooks.com, Website: www.gyanbooks.com

9 789357 131322